MW00649379

Searching
for
Dandelion Greens

poems

Valarie Hastings

Winner of the **STEVE KOWIT POETRY PRIZE 2020**

GARDEN OAK PRESS
RAINBOW, CALIFORNIA

Garden Oak Press
1953 Huffstatler St., Suite A
Rainbow, CA 92028
760 728-2088
gardenoakpress.com
gardenoakpress@gmail.com

First published by Garden Oak Press on June 15, 2021

ISBN-13: 978-1-7350556-6-4

Library of Congress Control Number: 2021936280

Printed in the United States of America

The views expressed in this collection of poems are solely those of the poet and do not necessarily reflect the views of the Publisher, and the Publisher hereby disclaims any responsibility for them.

for my family

Contents

Remembrance of things past is not necessarily the remembrance of things as they were.

— MARCEL PROUST

Searching
for
Dandelion Greens

poetry

Valarie Hastings

Winner of the STEVE KOWIT POETRY PRIZE 2020

Art by Linda Haim Meadows

3

Geneology

At the moment of my birth my great grandmother
was in the middle of a dream about birds, dressed
in the white gown they buried her with on the day
of my grandmother's 16th birthday. These were colored
birds on a field's canvas, one red for each
of the 4 children who died, and blue ones
for the 8 who survived.
The field was flecked with light.

At the moment of my birth my grandmother
turned in her sleep and saw a town built
on the side of a sunlit hill where her people
had once lived, a silver river running alongside
and streets filled with girls who looked
like her mother.

At the moment of my birth my mother
was asleep as the slow drip of labor
flattened her dreams. She slept even as I
moved through her, the dark
valves of her heart beating, beating
into me.

At the moment of my birth it was dark
like the universe before
light   I swam through winged
shadows that thrummed the air
into a blaze of light
that filled
my lungs.

Searching for Dandelion Greens

Most people, that's kind of the universal command for stop. †

I have come to forage for memory
with my plain sack and knife.
Pulling up these tender roots, shaking loose the dark soil,
I know in my heart I was a girl once,
my grandmother beside me,
the blade clean and easy in my hand.
Summer mornings in a field with my grandmother,
the light buttered down into the trees.
I was a girl once.

Taraxacum in Latin,
Lion's teeth—dents de lion in French.
Alhundba' alkhudar in the most beautiful language,
language of home,

language of fields in summer.

We empty the sack of its green and gold—
flowers dancing in a sheen of oil,
toothy ragged leaves
color of bitter dream on the tongue.

Tell me, what do you bright-handed boys know
about loss?

Every child wants
to take a fist full of these cottony seed heads,
blow them into the wind,
watch their delicate dreams carried up
on the slipstream of longing—
every child wants a home.

Each morning my grandfather left a silver coin
beneath his pillow so that I would find it
when I came to make his bed. What does it mean
to dream of dandelions?
I read once it means multiplying into many
good things—seed, flower, fruit—
light carried back from the fields,
memory of silver warming in my hand.

A girl told me once no amount
of beauty
can replicate home.
I see you have laid down your knife: I remember
it is the universal language
of peace.
I see you have come to forage with me—do you know
my grandmother?
Here, I have a plain sack, a knife,
I open my arms to show you.

†August 2018 interview of a Georgia police officer after he had tased
an 87-year old grandmother with dementia who had emigrated from
Syria. She had gone into the woods with a paring knife to cut
dandelion greens.

State of Emergency

It's Fat Tuesday and I'm riding the *1 California* to work with the baby
Jesus on my lap stuck inside a King Cake. I'm already amped on a double

shot latte made by the scar-battered hands of a refugee from El Salvador
who drives Uber after his Starbucks shift is up, because he thinks his kid

can be a doctor here, in America, when I read the President's at Mar-a-
Lago, three weeks into the NATIONAL EMERGENCY, after returning

from a failed summit in Viet Nam, a place he visited last week for the first
time since bone spurs first impeded his travel to Southeast Asia. And it

reminds me that my father was there, in the Sixties, for three tours of duty
in a white-out place in his life he still doesn't talk about. Not exactly

a golf holiday, but he voted for him all the same. And this gets me
thinking, again, about the video of that kid on the National Mall in a red

MAGA hat staring down a Native American old enough to be his
grandfather and I can't figure it out, how an 11th grader knows an America

greater than the one he was born into. I try to keep these ideas
to myself, but I grew up in the Seventies and I don't want to go back

to shag carpet and my mother's avocado kitchen, my boyfriend's blue
leisure suit. Richard Nixon. So when I hear the Dow's already slid 467

points this week and, 775 days into the presidency, our President is still
talking about the size of his inauguration crowd I'm pretty confident

nothing much is going to change the state we're in here. It's been raining
for three weeks solid after the fires almost incinerated us, because we

apparently forgot to rake our leaves. Some say it's like something out of
the Old Testament, this rain, and I pat the little cake on my lap and say it's

ok, because I kind of see their point. Folks just aren't turning their cheeks
like they used to. They're trading eyes and teeth for crack cocaine on

these sidewalks while we keep our heads in the down position on this bus,
ear buds in, our devices up. We're rolling over rivers of vomit out there.

Needles. Human feces mixed with rain. Bodies hunkered and cold behind
sheets of plastic. Yesterday I walked to work and saw a woman seated in

the middle of the sidewalk in a wheelchair with a potted tree roped
to her hand like a pet as the storm rolled over her, and I didn't even stop.

The woman sitting next to me on this bus is reading a story about Christ's
Blood on her phone. I'm reading about protests last weekend over a 22-

year old boy, same age as my own, who got blown away by eight rounds, six of those in the back, in his grandma's backyard because two cops

mistook his phone for a gun. I want to tell my fellow bus rider the baby inside this cake is plastic and made not in love but in China, that he's

painted gold because it's easier than trying to choose between black and white. That opioid deaths now exceed traffic fatalities in this country.

That we've lost our capacity for astonishment. The average bullet travels 1700 mph. That's more than twice the speed of sound. This means that

bullet can hit your kid before he even hears it. The news feed on my phone cheers me on, says our universe is expanding faster than it should

be. It doesn't have to tell me we are just like those dark-brimmed galaxies. The farther apart we are the faster we fly away from each other.

If Joy Were a Hit and Run

(from *The Top 10 Questions to Ask After a Hit and Run*)

Can you explain in your own words what happened?

> We were searching for fossils. Slippery, slimy,
> emerald-cool water pouring over the smooth stones
> in the creek behind my friend Sonja's house in those after school
> afternoons that would come to mean so much, learning to trust
> the feel of moss underfoot.

Can you identify the color, make, model?

> A red-muscled car speeding into the dazzled star struck
> summer of my seventeenth year with a boy whose
> name I no longer recall, one hand on the wheel
> the other on my bare knee, but also this: the unexpected
> discharge of light from gut straight into thrilled pistons
> of the heart when my father drove me fast over
> that certain curvature in the road on the way home.

> A joy ride we called it.

What were you doing before it hit you?

> I was thinking about a silk moth I saw in Big Sur
> on a July night in my forties with a complete stranger.
> Our paths crossed. We spoke no words, besotted
> by such invertebrate beauty, wings opened in a giant
> fan beneath damp porch light, the only sound our shared
> breath. We moved closer to consider the intricate
> hieroglyphics on its chiseled back, the hours and hours
> it must have taken its maker to paint them on,
> the rippled waves of color passing through us both,
> white, red, tan. Why is this what I remember?

Where are you now?

> Open the book. It tells us to rejoice in the land
> or was it the Lord   that night in my father's kitchen
> when he said into the phone, *I don't like people*
> *that are happy* right now or was it, *I don't trust*
> *happy* anymore? I meant to write it down
> but no longer know
> the feel of his arms around me.

Were there any witnesses?

> A grove of Eucalyptus watched from inside their green dreadlocks.
> Later, a storm came up over the Pacific, a curtain of wet steel
> that struck the windshield in silver sparks.   It felt like something
>   could happen.

What did you do afterward?

> I lay down on my back and looked
> at the stars. My God, the stars.

Is there anything else I should know?

> I snorkeled in a blue-green lagoon with a man I loved.
> I was afraid in the water at first but he held my hand inside
> his own as we submerged and the heat that burned down
> from all the coronas of the sun filled
> my lungs with light,
> made me see how
> I could breathe
>   underwater.

When Pigs Could Fly

The first wave came in undulating V-formations, piglets tiny as pugs drifting over streets in Minneapolis, Washington in late spring. Later, pot bellies could be seen overhead like jumbo jets, followed, some say, by great Palawan bearded sows all the way from the Asian archipelago. These were long-haul flights, miracles really, island-hopped across the Pacific to San Francisco, Walnut Creek. The people were afraid, at first, shut their doors, closed their blinds so as not to be judged by pigs passing outside their windows. But they began to notice how the pigs worked, in pairs, the way they circled their pen mates as each first sprouted wings, the pierce of feather and bone through such soft flesh painful but shouldered so bravely, and even as they transformed, the pigs remained true to themselves, compassionate, cheerful even, some opening the gates of their captivity to let the others out, a small passel at first, then the unstoppable droves of youngsters pushing through in places like Sioux City Iowa, Northfield Minnesota, Clinton North Carolina. They self-taught take-off and landing techniques, giving themselves names like Zoomer, Barky and Mad Max, always clean and fond of order. The tide began to change and there was a move to take the word "porker" out of the dictionary entirely, while the farmers stood agape, sounders of swine taking flight over their still-frozen fields and over the towns of helmeted cops who we had stopped calling "pigs," who we had stopped calling "cops" because they too were humbled and awed by what they saw in the sky. But there were also the bacon lovers and pulled pork eaters, the sausage and scrapple dreamers, the "other white meat" wanters who started their own movement, "when Hell freezes over," who objected to the removal of words from the past, those who were so fearful of change they could no longer parse nuance between black-spotted and pink. How could they be blamed for what others had eaten before them? And what then about the others—next it would be the bovines, the salmon, deer and cocks in their strutting red and yellow feathers seeking reparation. It was a dark time difficult for us to imagine, so long before we were born, when the whole world was locked down, pulled apart, afraid of dying, a time when mothers told their own daughters, *There will come a day when we part ways, over which news channel you watch.* Anger burned. And the land was a rage of promise. The mothers and fathers who had lost so much, grandmothers, grandfathers, sisters, brothers, aunts, uncles whose contract with this world was broken, dreams caught in the throat, they were afraid too of how things repeat but never change. But then the pigs flew, they kept flying, day after day that year, it was irrefutable, the fact of their earth-bound bodies lifted up over the darkened houses, flying! There were some who said it would never happen.

Love Poem in a Pandemic

We escape today w/a full tank & nowhere
to go, you driving hard through a spring rain into the Presidio
where the ragged fairytale trunks of Eucalyptus are gathered
like something new,
silvered leaves taking flight, flaunting
their freedoms. Now look
at the wiper blades, how
they flex their mechanical muscle over the windshield
striped blue with rain, clearing then blurring
our vision,
at these two red-tailed hawks
steadily circling a patch of light on the wet fields, how
you & I emerge on the empty highway
as though startled from a dark sleep,
the famous bridge half-appearing
from inside the rain-lit air like an unexpected force
luminous in the clear gray
of the afternoon. Crossing over,
the way our shoulders relax ever slightly, my breath
slowing, regulating for the first time all week,
like driving inside an abandoned cathedral,
its great red arc pushing into heaven as the road
spray washes over us. We take the Sausalito exit,
emptied of tourists, pull over & park, still vacuum-sealed
in our getaway machine,
the city's silence echoing back at us from across the bay,
blue-black & endless. Still there.
I kiss you then, your neck straining over
the seat belt and say something like,
This is really romantic & you say, Yes it is
& the heart's engines kick up again,
throw their butterfly wings into the belly.

The Lake is Undressing the Sky, Again

for J.T.

She is a silver hand quietly
undressing the sky,
all mineral hush, patience and blue breath.
She says, I get excited about the fabrics,
noon's velvet heat falling away.
An August storm waits, watches, before releasing
its clatter of tin spoons.
These green hills weren't even here this morning,
they were nothing more
than a necklace of trees in my hair.
She is a dark eye closing and we are rain-
lashed deep in pine because our tongues long
for sugar-dipped lemons from childhood,
unpacked from the basket, wax yellow in our hands.
I believe we still have all the time in the world, my love.
My teacher said, once, All my children loathe me.
They kept yelling, *Where is he? Where is he?*
He will come back as a new-born father
with a golden dog nestled
inside his lap, an agate
sphere of rain
on his tongue, a kind of forgiveness.
The lake is undressing, again, the afternoon
and we are children at the pearled collars of her shore
licking the last sweet molecules of joy
from our lips.

Coming Over Altamont Pass
After Three Days on the Road

The foothills are yawning—
rolling shoulders seductively unaware

of the way their golden pelts
shimmer in early October. Giant

white turbines rise up ahead
like triple-armed aliens milling

light & who dropped
these half dozen grazing cattle

here, like something out of a Dutch
painting, for contrast and effect,

the trucks alongside me oblivious,
humming. I swear

Rembrandt's walking that hill to my right,
thigh-deep in California

needle grass, working out
the brush strokes for later tonight, back

in his marbled-wood room in Amsterdam
with Saskia, cut flowers spilling

loosely from a small blue vase
beside the bed,

while I am here, time-traveling inside
my little machine,

roaring down 580 with a bellyful
of coffee, on my way home to you.

Seeing My Mother
Through the Pandemic

The day she calls
my office, she's kneeling before
four or five boxes of bank
records from twenty-five
years ago. Hasn't thrown
them out after two moves
because she hasn't yet checked
each to be sure the bank
got it right.

Later,
she leaves me
a voicemail message.
She's been going through the boxes,
the stacks
of cancelled checks,
the boxes
that are keeping her from sleeping, keeping
her from moving
into her new life and tells me, her delight sudden,

"I found one I wrote you for a hundred dollars"—I see the words
as she speaks them to me into the phone—"*Val's—twentieth—birthday*,"
written over the bottom of the long-ago cancelled check in her looping
left-handed cursive. "I've pulled this one out, to send you,"
she says,

this connection
between us
made through a kind of time machine,
my voicemail box,
linking us
to a moment when we were still
in the past,
yet to be recorded.

•

An attendant is pushing my mother's body in a wheelchair through
security, her hands clutching the leather purse I gave her 20 years
ago, held together now with safety pins and thread, stuffed
with folded scraps of Christmas wrapping and ribbon she's taken
out of the recycle bag in my apartment to save for next year, a half
peanut-butter sandwich she will neither eat nor throw away, two crisp
dollar bills she made me get from the bank to tip the attendant and four
unopened packs of Marlboro (lights), her snow-white head bobbing just
above the back of the chair. She hands her license to the TSA agent
who laughs about something she says, something I can't hear, and she
turns then, waves back at me like a girl going somewhere, maybe
home.

•

My mother was a girl going somewhere once. Rome, once, 1953,
a college trip, drinking Vodka martinis with two boys from Maryland
who'd come into the cool dark of the *Bar Florida* to find her there, before
she was my mother, legs crossed on a tall stool in her Italian sandals,
smoking. "Those martinis were good," the first she'd tasted.
She cannot recall their names, the boys, yet remembers perfectly
how she ditched the Vatican that day, trading two packs of American
cigarettes for a painting of a black-hatted cardinal in cassocks
cascading over a series of church steps in smooth red angles, a painting
that hung my whole life in our foyer in the suburbs. I can't help but feel
there's a clue here for me in this picture of my mother, that this
is somehow who she's always been, like ethyl alcohol,
my mother in her purest form,

the same woman who paid for the poetry books and
a leather-bound journal for me but could never bring
herself to read any poem I wrote. They remain folded, sealed
in their white envelopes on a desk,

like the skirt I made the summer I was twelve,
its pattern delft blue and white, the fabric crisp
and my stitching on the Singer uneven and imperfect, the skirt
a gift I'd worked at for weeks, laid out
all these years so carefully
beneath layers and layers of white
tissue paper in her dresser, an entire drawer devoted
to it, smoothed back
by her hands, perfectly
preserved like a still
life she could never touch,
never tried on.

continued

●

For my twentieth birthday my mother made a chocolate cake, something
she rarely did and drove with it in the passenger seat of her Buick
the three hours to my dorm room where I told her the housing lottery
had paired me with a black girl my age from Virginia the next year.
Her unexpected fury at this unacceptable situation   details speeding

up in time now, coat over her arm, back
of her head, dark hair pulled tight
into her bun, the cake on a table, smack
of the door, the vacuum silence left behind
and the energy inside my body electric and sudden as a bolt,
my arms like something newly detached
as they smashed through the layers of cake.

Oh, the sound
that made.

            ●

We live now three
thousand miles apart
in quarantine, speak
once a day b/c I call
her. No internet,
no face time. No-
body. Did you take
your Sertraline?
Blood pressure
pills? Are you
wearing
gloves
when you go out
for cigarettes?
The mask
I made you?
Do you
have enough
food
love
air
            (Can

            I

            do

            something

            (anything)

            to help

            you?)

18

We stay close
to what is not.

Our country burns.
Our President
hides.
She says, I feel like I am 83 years old,

says,

I don't know what/
who I am
anymore.
I see the table
where my beautiful mother sits and speaks these words to me,
                                        stretched end
to end with the junk
mail she needs,
needs to read
before she can release it,
to the recycle bin,
grocery store receipts
that must be checked,
the suitcase from the last time
I saw her here, with me,
unopened
upstairs in her room,
the 1980s suits and pumps
from her once life pulled
from the closet, strewn
across the bed in layers,
silk skirts,
empty jacket
sleeves
once-tended plaids
and beloved bow tie blouses
carrying the scent
of old perfume
in a heap where she sleeps
because
maybe,
maybe this week
she'll give them up
to Goodwill,

continued

19

maybe she'll
call pest control today,
Fox News saying
No, No, No
on the kitchen's little flat screen,
buzzing
into the threads
of optic cables
pulled between us,
and I wonder about all
we never say,
if
I will ever see my mother again,
if

she saw me that afternoon
in the rearview
mirror,
running,
running into the parking lot
as the car pulled away,
windows rolled up,
my face wet, welted red,
those sweet smashed hunks
of chocolate
clinging, clinging
to my hands.

Blue Anthem

It is a night in Tucson in the Sixties,
my mother dressing me in a powder blue jacket
soft as rabbit's fur. The scent of her neck as
she carries me dream heavy to the backseat,
my father a shadow behind the wheel.

It is the color of my bones
as she strokes my back on a Sunday at the breakfast table
before she leaves
a color that begins in the mouth
and descends into the red sleeve of the throat where it churns
its electric sparks of grief and flows hot into the dark
hole of the belly.

Later it is the vein in my white thigh
the nurse stabs with the needle
for the procedure to fix
the electric impulse of my heart

and the indigo thread inside the volcanic rock
my beloved carries down a mountainside
for me.

It is a ruined church at twilight
where we stopped the car
to listen to the blue hum of summer,

the stone in the wedding band,
the bruise of my mother's eye.

It is the color of my child's eyes
of my mother's, my father's, my own,

the blue night gown grown thin but familiar
inside the icy sheets of childhood,
the sapphire molecule of blood.

It is the snow outside my mother's door now,
hardened by moonlight,
suspended somewhere between flesh and marble.

That color.

Photograph of My Parents, 1971

The summer my father returns from Viet Nam
he spends time with my mother and me,
an entire afternoon pressed into the front seat
of her sky-blue Cutlass. Thigh-deep in hot
white vinyl, we see the White House
the Washington Monument, all three buildings
of the Smithsonian through open car windows.
We eat egg salad and olive sandwiches on a curb
behind the Rayburn. My mother chain smokes.

At the Zoo the Bengal cats are sleeping. I devour
him whole with my Instamatic. Chest, knees
crotch, bones and all, the orange light
hanging on him still like spun sugar
in Southern heat. He is mid-sentence when I
"1-2-3" snap the button, the wet July trees
pouring their shade into his half-opened mouth,
words I no longer remember caught there,
invisible as dust in tigers' bellies.

It is late afternoon when they stand together
for one photograph, awkward as teenagers
before the prom. I frame the great white
dome behind them, Tecumseh's spire
threaded neatly through the hive of my mother's
lustrous hair. I am unprepared for the sudden
bareness of her arms, winter-pale in a pink
sleeveless dress. She flashes her nervous
girl-smile to his new, forever-altered face.
Years later I will notice how he grabs her
hand just as the shutter closes, slightly
blurring their fingers together, forever.

Geese, 1967

for my father

Recess, early spring. Frozen fields asleep
beside the schoolyard, their icy husks

rising up around us like hollowed men, air still
cold & hard in our chests.

A game of four-square in play, slap
of India red rubber on black tarmac when our teacher cries,

Look up! Above us a sudden, noisy V of geese cutting
the steel plate of sky. I keep a secret

in my woolen coat pockets.
My father is flying too, somewhere deep

inside poofs
of Napalm cloud & green jungle sky.

I am six years old with a secret
for my father.

Recess, early spring. Air like green
ice inside the red pockets

of my lungs. Blue plate of sky
& these white birds, daddy,

their forlorn calls fading,
falling across the fields,

coming home.

Learning to Fish

My father bursts across the pages
of that year in green fatigues and combat
boots. He drops
from helicopters,
disappears
into jungles
as suddenly
as he teaches me to thread
the hook with a nightcrawler.
On Saturdays
I polish his boots black with a horsehair brush
for a half dollar, call him, *Sir*, sink
long and deep inside
his praise. That summer
I cast out
into the small yard
for hours,
learning
the arc of the line
its shimmer in heat,
the feel of a rod
in my grip.
I bring him stories he asks me
to write and worms
freshly dug from the garden, spread
across the table, the smell of raw
earth and rain clinging to my hands
through dinner. He always says,
More. I fall headfirst
through
first grade,
shivering in the brief
light of those days,
a plumb golden
thing waiting
to be scooped up,
enjoyed whole.

Steam

My mother would sing
when she ironed and
I could almost believe
she was happy.

The heft and heated glide
of the iron in her hand,
my father's clean, white
shirts in a basket

beside her, sprinkled
with water. There was a simple
satisfaction in pressing
pleats and collars,

erasing the wrinkles
of empty shirtsleeves,
a job well done,
the shirts starched

and lifted up
on their hangars
to be opened
like gifts.

Before the milkman refused
delivery
to the divorcee
with a baby girl,

before
we packed
the Oldsmobile up and left
that year behind for good
there was this—

the sweet smell
of cotton yielding
to steam,
the plane

of hot steel smoothing
it over like a skin on the board,
my mother's small, sure
voice.

Jurisdiction

The night you call me I drop
everything and come.

I find you sitting still
facing the door

in the Mexican restaurant
on the corner,

as we'd planned—if
things got worse—

tattered
backpack on your lap, nails chewed

down to their quicks.
We know what

to do
this time, an officer leading us

into the clean lit
room,

the kind of room with hard
chairs where they sit

survivors
down, ask them

if they would like cream
or sugar, a blanket.

You file the report
in your own steady hand,

dispassionate as Kafka
giving these uniformed strangers

just the facts, how
your father had swung hard

into oncoming traffic, twice
on the bridge, and again

over the County line.
We've got jurisdiction then,

one of them says.
You leave out

the word "whore" in what
you tell them

and all the words
for fear and flight, the line of headlights

coming at you, how
they burned your eyes,

telling them only
what he said

about
wanting to go down

together
what you said

about not
wanting

to die nothing
about the motion

in your gut as the car
flung your mind

against the hard of night,
against all you were

made into,
here in this room calmer

than a crisis negotiator walking
the leaper back

from the ledge,
catching

the baby tossed
from the burning building,

focused
as an EMT

checking vitals
at the scene of the crash.

Gulf Shores

for E. Laughlin

That first summer
she collected shells,
bucketsful of milk bone,
fossil shards,
tiny cathedrals bleached white,
their helical folds
dialed deep as the inner ear
and sea glass that carried
the broken light and heat from that time
pitch perfect,
the dream-colored song of it,
50 years on.

O, Alabama,
did I tell you?
Not the crack
of iron in the sky
that day,
the eye of the storm
following me from room
to room.
Not the color
of cloth I moistened
on tipped
toes
at the sink
but the sound
of her moaning
I have carried
with me
all these years.

The Strand

It's old magic again
On a Monday in October
Out on Portstewart Strand
Where I wait beneath the light
As I have in dreams
And in half-dream you come,
To drive me fast into the night
Through a tunnel deep with sedge
And wild grass that opens
To the sea. You have been here
Before.

Show me everything   you swear
You'll light up the sea
For my eyes
But your headlights
Are paler than moonbeams
On parallel paths
That fall short and dissolve into black,
Leave me only to imagine
The waters beyond.

So that all I remember of you this night
Is sedge and darkness
And breath on the window
So thick I never see your eyes
Only the heat of your voice
In blindness
I memorize your body
Again
This last time

And tell you
My heart is a storm
Only you have seen.

Psalm

Sing me the field of my seventh year
of the ash and pine and willow
at the yard's dark edges
Sing me each shadow
in the forest of my grandfather's life
the POW camp, the coronet, the boy
whose life he saved
each star he named for me
in summer
Sing me back
to cherry blossomed trees in Niigata
to the bombs that brought him home
Back to the orchard of my mother's childhood
the path scattered in pink on her birthday
the fists full of apple blooms carried home
to her mother
Sing me grief and piss and heat
Sing me the labors of our fathers in jungles
the hovering and chop of blades
in the air
Sing me the cavalry
the horse
the tank
Sing me the child who survives
the slaughter
Sing me the failed banks and the bear markets and their fur coats
from Bergdorf's
the pack of gum I stole
when I was five
and the smack of mint in my teeth
of the bottle hidden behind the Hoover
Sing me venal sin red vermouth and sweet cherries
in a dark paneled confessional
where my dead have kneeled
before I was born
Sing me the casket
the hardness of patella
on stone
of marble and prayer
on Sundays
Sing me a smoke on the back stoop
after the dishes have dried
in the early evening as the crickets come on

Sing me a silver strand
of my grandmother's hair
beneath my pillow
Sing me the color of my boy's
on fire with field light
the smashed fist of stars
in summer dark
Sing me home

Letter to a Dead Poet
on Good Friday, 2020

for P.L.

Listen. The world has become so quiet it has stopped
vibrating. You can hear the fishes speak. Today I read
the Archbishop of New Orleans dropped holy water
from a WWI biplane, his wooly red cassocks flowing
over Kenner, Gretna, the French Quarter — when I first did it,
he said, the water, it came back on me & then I got it
right. Isn't it just the way it was when you were last here
with me? Something always blowing back
in your eye, waiting & waiting for the road
to rise up with you? We're talking big
gestures down here now, the kind you love, falling
scattershot over the dying. Sister. I'm afraid
the fog's come in to stay here in the north,
inching over the roofs like ghosts who move
too slowly through my sleep. O, widow, Bohemian
Queen. Tell me, was it heart failure or heart
break? Listen. I swear the Rose Café's
still open on the corner of Rose & Main.
We can grab coffee & talk about the first time you knew
you were in love, roses in your arms along Venice Beach,
sky blushing over you, the first time you said to me, Yes. This
is a poem. Teacher. It's been too long. That night
in Malibu, our hearts still alive reading Pound,
Pound! My good wine nearly drunk
& the pink moon howling back at us over the hillsides.
We could have gone on forever. Mother. Please do not
look back. That house burned to the ground last year,
those hills black as bad weather now. Last night
I found a book of poems a dead man loaned me,
his favorites still marked with cut-out red
ribbons of paper, the looping cursive of his name inked
onto the front flap & I understood something then
about the velocity of darkness, that there was no one
to give them back to. I awaken like a phantom in my home
& watch the streetlamp outside the room pour
its incandescent sadness into the fog, the fog
swarming the lamp's haloes of light like insects
& it scares me. Friend—inside my small backyard
on an evening not unlike this one now I did something
like genuflection into the dirt, my knees sighing
beneath me, my hands sinking into the chard
with its extravagant leaves, the lettuces all in a row
singing out their names to me as to a lover from the shadows —
Lolla Rosa, Rose d'Hivers, Blush Batavian —

32

I touched them each for blessings,
the fur along the shoots
of squash, the yams' mottled hides, kissing
the rings of sweet peas running up the trellises in their purple robes
like ambitious bishops. Please
   give my love to your old man. Let him know
I still have his Patchen
& read it sometimes.

Letter to My Self from 16 Summers Ago

Flying into Williamsport the airport emerges like a small bright cross
burned onto asphalt, the moon half eaten away and my son beside
me: Mine for two weeks. The next morning, over the farmhouse, such
a sight: three then five then a dozen hawks dropping

shadow crosses across the lawn. They circle our upturned faces in
lamentation or as welcome, who knows, but tonight they're gone,
just like that, replaced, by a murder of crows scratching the filmy edge
of evening damp with their calling. He's reading *The Wind in the Willows*

but hasn't gotten far inside this kingdom of my once childhood
with too many things to do. A horse. A swim. Ride the mower again
around the barn's moat. Climb every tree in the yard. Play
Gin Rummy with grandma all day. The breeze he says, with authority,

"Comes all the way from Toronto" because he heard it on the radio.
Radio? Here, even weather reports flicker with the extraordinary. We eat
corn from my mother's garden and tomatoes that hold an entire day's
heat. After dinner we swim, the length of our bodies moving blue

through chlorine water and I see my son bug-eyed in goggles, the blaze
of sun lowering itself into the giant pine behind us, its flash
of late summer glory in the upper branches, flaming next into the apple
and ash trees. All of it sharp as a knife. The silence of water pouring

through my ears, the remains of the day fading along the hem
of field. And the vision of child, light, tree, sky. All of it without
sound. The whole world emptied out and reconfigured now
to these elements. We are alone. We come into it alone

and we leave alone. At the end it is the body alone with itself. Each
of us given that country all to ourselves. But before that, and this
is what I need to tell you, before that, we have all of this, all of it.
Simply there, for the taking.

My Flight Needed a Flight

My flight needed a flight you know how you get situated and strapped in and then they bring the little cart round and tell you they don't take cash

anymore and you don't have a card now because you gave up credit like you should give up wine except you love the stuff and it helps you get

through the flying itself and then the flight is in the air without the flight of wine but you knew all along there was never going to be any of those cute

little thimble glasses they give you on long hauls in business class because you're traveling to see your elderly mother on Miles and therefore you're

in steerage right now smashed up against the overweight insurance salesman and his wife next to you and their huge baby in a lap seat and

you're thinking the baby should be in a carry on it's so big and won't fit under the seat so I mean I'm on exactly *that flight* for more or less five

and half hours of my life and from the aisle seat I happen to notice 29c and 31c are both watching Tom Cruise in of course an action movie but

the two of them are at different points in the same movie On the little screen at 31c Tom Cruise is crashing a small jet and handing a package to

a brown skinned boy and further up in 29c Tom's wearing his signature brilliant sparkling smile kissing his blonde wife and his pink skinned child

like a little flight within a flight within a flight and it feels like all of us are hurtling toward the same conclusion here but you know life might be no

more than this a series of images some connected or maybe memory is just like a movie here I am kissing my boy who skinned his knee outside the

small apartment we shared when he was 5 and behind or just up ahead is my divorce or maybe the death of my favorite dog Bear while the man in

31c is just getting to the wife and 29c is watching another man in a pay phone making a call before getting on a plane and I think how marvelous

that I can sit inside this machine tearing across the country at 500 miles an hour with a big baby kicking my seat and call up the memory of my dad's

new wife my beautiful stepmother on a Saturday morning in 1967 at the black leather table that was our dining table then and would become a card

continued

35

table in another life and hear her say clear as a bell I can make BLTs for lunch the words falling just like they did then over the uneaten strips of

bacon on a platter She is smiling at my dad with her frosted tresses cropped short and flipped up at the bottoms she's all of 24 to my 6 wearing

flowered hip huggers well ok I made up that detail but not my dad's face looking at her the way he did all bemused and fit and I am trying to sort

out what he's not saying and wondering at the same time why my own mom never fried bacon for me whether it was because she didn't know

how or that she couldn't afford it or that she just couldn't be bothered and 51 years on that BLT I mean it seems extravagant sexy even and I have no

idea why I even remember it but my biggest problem at this moment is how to balance my journal and pen on the wobbly little table you get on

these flights that you pull up from the side arm like a clunky gun hat trick of metal the surface stuck with dried up juice and peanut salt and Bill the

insurance guy next to me wants to know What are you writing in the journal the one my true love gave me for Christmas that came all the way

from Paris France from a guy named Thibault I had to order it myself of course because my true love can't speak or write French worth crap but I

pretended to unwrap it with a surprised Christmas face while my sullen 23-year-old boy simultaneously handed me a book about raising

happy men in the year 2019 and I say you know in my best coach seat voice to Bill in response to his question that when I told my dad I wanted

to be a writer he told I needed to have experience before I could do that and I could no more have challenged him as much as I worshipped the

look of approval on his face than I could've grown a boy's body right there in front of him so I went to law school and hated it so much I

practiced law and hated it until I loved it and it consumed me like a jealous mistress and became all that I was and then I found miraculous love with

my new husband because that's what my ex always calls him you know Your New Husband even though we've been married going on 20 years

now and so I started to write again I tell Bill and I thought about how little time is left about how a BLT can be like a cartoon sandwich until you eat

36

it so that's why I write and Bill takes this in and his big baby in his lap
stares at me with huge green grey eyes and I think I'm beginning to get to

the gold here or the quick of some answer that has evaded me before like
why my mom didn't fry bacon and maybe I will remember to ask her

about it when I see her if we ever get off this plane and I recall then that
trip when I listened to a.m. radio on my Walkman flying to New York

hearing the disc jockeys burp up into my headphones and disappear in
seconds the twang of a song two three notes of it over Nevada or maybe

Utah then gone like time travel everything everything happening at the
same time

Beating Nixon's Doctor's Daughter
at Dodgeball

for Ann

The year they moved out of the tenement
(b/c her mother liked to call it that)
Ruby was 9 & the Seventies had arrived dressed
in bell bottoms. The new kitchen was avocado
green & they had a blender.
Anything was possible.

Ruby felt the texture of that time like corduroy & suede.
She missed her father in that new house, felt
the missing of him like a nerve she hid from her mother
on account of what had led them here, which did not so much
mar her mother's beauty as create a point
of conversation for the new neighbors who'd never
been in the presence of a divorced woman before, much less
one that looked and thought like Ruby's mother.

Ruby knew that moving here meant a lot to her mother,
that she needed to love it here like she loved her mother
& that this meant she had to make friends with the gum-
chewer across the street whose father was Richard Nixon's
doctor. Later Ruby would find this was funny but in 1971,
Ruby didn't know she was living in interesting times.

One Sunday the girl across the street got splashed
across the Washington Post shaking Brezhnev's hand
("I'll never wash it again"), with her father on the tarmac
at Dulles, him in his suit & her looking smug just like
she always did, the same girl who said, "Well,
at least *I* have a father" when Ruby was beating her
at dodgeball, the same afternoon Ruby hit her hard
in the center of her tits with the ball.

The same girl whose mother was the Girl Scout Leader
on Thursdays & took her girls to swim club after school
on Wednesdays while Ruby's worked single mother days
& tried dating men who were not Ruby's father who called
Ruby *sweetie* b/c they didn't have a clue about a 10-year old,

they just wanted time w/her mother and not her *suitcase,*
which is what Ruby's mother had started to call her by 1972,
& Ruby could see by then how she was a little like that blue
Samsonite with the fake pebbled leather, the one she carried
every summer when her mother packed her up and sent her off
to "your father's family."

Ruby was the bag & she took the bag, & that was funny,
which helped when the plane door slammed shut & the two
of them, Ruby & her mom, became separate people
for three months until late August when Ruby returned,
& they resumed their life together in the suburbs.

When she turned 11, the President's doctor offered to take Ruby
to the father-daughter dance at school while Ruby's mother stayed
home studying for the LSAT & the other girls stared at her or at least
she thought they did in the cafeteria decorated with balloons in a dress
she'd borrowed with her fake dad and his real daughter as though
they were sisters.

Ruby ran into that girl once after they'd both moved away
& the girl started in on latch key kids as though they
had just been speaking about it, as though it was
a gateway drug. Ruby understood then the girl had wanted
something juicy—how had they managed all those
years w/o a father, without a husband for God's sake?

& Ruby remembered then how the girl's face
bunched up in surprise when the red ball hit her
that afternoon, after it left the curl of her 12-year old arm,
the pure energy of that moment, the way the light hit
the trees and how someone's mother came out
and yelled *stop* as though anyone could turn back time
& Ruby took a breath then exhaled slow & said,
Yeah. My mom. Wasn't she amazing?

Lost Horses

I wanted a horse the year I turned 7 and believed in the power of my desire to make it real. My grandma had a serious collection of brooms back then. Sitting on her stoop behind a curl of Parliament smoke, she would watch me ride them across the yard in my purple princess costume like something wild she could not fully contain.

I named them each, spoke quietly to them like you should do with horses, and watched them drink from the starry pond with friends no one else could see. At night I tied them up to sleep so they couldn't leave. I hadn't counted on the garbage man

thinking they'd been left for him to take, which he did, one winter morning while we slept. There were loud discussions and the herd was replaced with a single new broom from A&P she locked in a cabinet. I was given a stick pony with a stuffed vinyl head and a red bow around its neck that looked nothing like the ones I'd lost.

I had four teeth pulled that spring and Ma drove from the city where she lived and took me to see *The Horse in the Gray Flannel Suit*. It wasn't much of a story, about a girl and a horse named *Aspercel* which was funny to say out loud but no one in the movie was yelling at each other or leaving, and

it felt good to be sitting there with Ma, our butts smashed together deep inside those plush seats at the Campus Theater, the scent of her hair close enough for me to taste. We went to the dairy for lunch that day where we had black cows and Ma bought me a post card with a picture

of some palominos in a pasture and I told her I'd put it under my pillow at night when she was gone. We went to Halfway Dam afterward and hunted for salamanders because she'd done so as a girl and then I forgot the postcard on the riverbank and Ma wouldn't buy me another to replace it so as to teach me a lesson I already knew.

When Ma got in her car to leave that Sunday my chest started making that heaving sound I couldn't control and my grandparents looked embarrassed with their arms at their sides like they'd seen all of this before. That summer I asked for a real horse for my 8th birthday and I

didn't care that I got a pair of tiny silver pins in the shape of horses instead, two in case I lost one, but I didn't care because I left with Ma in her big blue car and didn't need to look back.

I Would've Had
Some Other Version of You, That's All.

My mother says this at the dinner table,
after the fourth or fifth glass of wine is emptied
and the light in the room has turned sad. She's
talking about the dark, rich boy from Italy, the one she
should've married. I already know this story,
how he followed her everywhere that year
like a dog. My father would never
have done that. But she'd already met my father.
And there were other considerations.
Like washing machines. It seems Italy hadn't yet discovered
Whirlpool. It was 1954, and she couldn't do it.
Just couldn't imagine that kind of life. Clothes in the sink.
Making love in broken Italian the rest of her days.
Learning to cook pasta.

I think of those other versions of myself.
The darker-haired children she would've had.
The shape of their eyes, hands formed from other
grandmothers'. And I think of my son,
the gift of a bad marriage.
Unrepeatable.

Fast Food

They lined up those kids down the road from me,
lined them up in the back freezer in November, beside
the unopened bags of buns, the iced boxes of meat
patties while they emptied the tills. Then shot every one
of them on the night shift. I was working Gino's-KFC then
three nights a week in the 10th grade, dressed head to toe
in a tight red polyester uniform, silly hat with the company
logo pinned to my head like a fast food stewardess calling
out orders over a microphone up front to the pimpled boys
in back who fried the frozen chicken parts and dunked
fist-sized cherry pies in vats of oil, our faces shining holy
and young in florescent light and recycled grease, the first
job any of us had had. My mother made me quit when
the story ran as though mass murder might be something
I'd catch. But that summer we'd drive home after midnight,
all of us in our borrowed parents' cars burning rubber past
Gino Marchetti's GIANT BANQUET ON A BUN sign, blasting
Blinded by the Light from our open windows, racing each other
into all the darkness that lay ahead, feeling alive for the first time.

Que Será, Será

Doris Mary Anne Kappelhoff, 1922-2019

I knew her before she was a virgin. — OSCAR LEVANT

Before I was celluloid. Flammable. Precious. Easily
molded and shaped. Expensive. Before
I was a virgin.
Before
the girl next door opened
the door. I was

this:
a girl who wanted a husband who loved me. A house-full
of children. I made

39 pictures. Belted out
650 hits. Had my palms, the tiny spike heels and
pointed toes

of my pumps pressed
into concrete at Grauman's Chinese,
a star on the walk of fame.

And three marriages before I hit 27. God gave me
a voice. All I did was use it. I believed everything
happens for a reason. When I wore

the top-half of a pair of Weldon heart-printed pajamas
for a two-week shoot they told me
it was the sexiest thing I ever did.

Can you imagine?
Flannel, bare legs   no stockings. Before
my third

bilked me. Or didn't. Before I kicked my fourth
out. It was still all I wanted after my son died.
And when they changed the number

of syllables
in my name to three, took two years
off my birthday. Even after my body was published
like a book of song, a perfect hour
glass with a cocktail. 36 26 36. When
the hours and the numbers mattered. I had

a voice.
I used it. What
ever

46

will be? America never wants
to look too deep.
Did anyone care that in the end I was happiest
with my dogs? America loves
her stars
bright

& bold. Empty but chesty. Give us back
the perky
blonde from *The Man Who Knew Too Much*

when I already knew
too much. More than I let on. The honey-husky
notes carried out of my throat a kind of joy,

Jimmy with his *Mr.- Smith-Goes-to-Washington-It's-a-Wonderful-
Life*-gee-wiz face: my complete foil.
Didn't every boy

want to have a mom just like her?
Didn't every housewife think,
I can be her in a pill box

hat,
with hunky Rock
in the split

screen of *Pillow Talk*.
Another champagne chaser, please. You could be or be with
that girl. Sex

glittering under the surface, not quite
forbidden.
Something else altogether. Approachable and incendiary. Combustible.
I gave you that too.

America,
you hate watching your stars waste   the long
fade. The recluse film goddesses. I wanted
to want
what will be.

Now   let it burn.

Between Places

Behind the barn
apples
languish in grass
knee-deep. Bees sing
the heat. The trees
suffer it quietly. Tonight
a troika of black horses
will tear across the lawn,
too beautiful for sleep.
For now, pears lie
spent in the weeds.
In my hand,
a photo of my son at six,
hair on fire with field light.
His eyes say,
Leave the stars in the pond
the almond orchards
like torches in bloom.

Stay here with me
and live.

A Matter of Age

"Old eggs." He says this with a kind face,
a voice like a Midwestern plain. Empty,
expansive. Nothing you could have done
differently. This comes as a relief,
knowing it is simply a matter of age,
that we have not become the kind of people
to whom bad things happen. At 5:30 a.m.
the splash of blood contained a color so vivid
I thought something inside me had popped.
A fanfare of red and pink streamers across
the bathroom tile and your bright red form
jettisoned. Elusive little fish, I fell asleep full
of your swimming last night and awoke
an old woman, the sound of your papa sobbing
softly in my hair.

The Story of Your Hands

after Mark Strand

I am in the Ash tree
in my grandfather's garden
and you have just arrived.
I feel summer well up
from the tree,
the steam
of light
from the fields.
The tomatoes have grown fat
as red
suns.
Pears drop
from their green
branches.
You are not aware of them
because you have just arrived.
The Ash
reminds you of something
you do not yet know.
There is a sadness
in the way the light
arranges itself across
your shoulders.
I believe you think
it is a sorrow
you were meant to wear.
I am so small, the Ash so
ordinary
I wonder why you've come at all.
I ask,
Why are you wearing that ridiculous hat?
You cannot answer.
You cannot see me
falling from the tree
or hear the small crack of bone
on the supple grass.
You are walking toward me for the first time
and do not know my story.
The music of locusts rises, falls.
I shall count the children
we will lose.
I shall lay them down on beds of mulch
moistened with our sleep.
But you have just arrived
and do not know the story of our children.

Come down, you say,
Lie with me
in the grass
and I will tell you the story
of my hands.
A blur of gnats
darkens the air around your hat.
Where did you get it?
You told me once
but I do not remember.
In a city far from here
you will rise in the night
and say,
Your existence keeps me
awake.
My mouth
will be a small wet womb
around these words.
You are walking toward me
for the first time.
You see the Ash
is winter silver
in August light.
Soon you will take off your hat.
Soon the tree will become your existence.
I feel the turning of sky
around each word we leave behind.
I know by the way you bring your hand
to your head and scratch
that you have seen me now.
I hear a spider in the leaves
and wonder, what secrets
have I overlooked?
You are walking toward me for the first time.
I feel your limbs falling
through my arms
like summer's weighted light.
Soon you will take off your hat.
Soon I will know the story of your hands.
You will look at me and say to yourself,
Now there is my future.
The light is arranging itself
across your shoulders
like a mantle.
There is nothing left
to be done.

The Shape of Dust

(Saharan Dust Cloud Arrives in North Texas, July 2018)

From the 17th floor, Dallas
Texas is the color of copper,
hazy light filtering over
her concrete bridges and freeways,
striations of dust spinning out to the south,
the triple digit heat trapped inside
her border like a ferocious animal,
the effect of a Saharan sandstorm carrying
itself like a refugee 5000 miles across the Atlantic
to this place on the map, where I
am holed up in a Marriott
working.

An olive-skinned boy walks out of my notebook,
out of the dust of childhood,
sits down beside me on the bed.
He spent years in the desert, selling Cokes to the Berber men,
icing them down in the back of a Deux Cheveaux,
each bottle of cold brown syrup and water
putting him one step closer to Europe.
The power of heat was a revelation to him,
the nights thin as rain.
He dreamed of his mother and
the faces of women, taking
what he could—
glimpse of a hennaed hand, cleavage
in a sandal,
the beauty and loneliness crushing
but that restaurant job in France just up
ahead.

He pulls out a deck of cards and
we play Ronda on the bed cover
like before.
As he deals
he remembers to me Timgad, crossing
the blue-green Aurès —
coming upon it for the first time
like a jewel in the sea of heat,
the sunken shadows of Roman roads calling him
forward into a ruined city embalmed in sand,
the stuff of dreams.
How I wanted to drown in the foreignness of it,
carved tombs flung open to the glittering light,
coins on the desert floor for the taking.

13,000 refugees cast out into the Algerian desert this year
left to navigate the sand seas and gold flecked hamada
with nothing
more
than a compass of stars.

A round number says something,
says nothing
about the shape of hope,
of dreams.

Outside my hotel room tonight
the sun slides down the glassy buildings
emptied of their human cargo,
windows on fire, half-drunk with heat.
The local papers are all over it,
the way dust bends the light—
We are in for some spectacular sunsets
Exotic they say, dangerous too.
Close your windows. Wear a mask. Stay
inside till it's moved on—
North Africa, here, in the Lone Star State,
her desert in our lungs—
as close as we'll ever get.

Last Flight Out

She's on duty at the Southwest ticket counter.
10:46 and I need the last flight out. Need
to get home. By the time I've pulled out my photo
ID, I know she's got a degree from St. John's,
substitute teaches in the afternoon, 11th graders
from the projects, that this education is theirs
to take. And how none of them hear her.
AmeriCorps taught her how to survive this world. She likes,
really likes, the photo on my driver's license,
tells me I should think about contact lenses.
Tapping a finger to her security badge, "Ms.
Alice Walker" speaks frankly. About hair.
Which cuts work. Which ones don't. She tells
those gang-bangers how much they're gonna make
flipping meat at Burger King. $5.25 an hour. She
writes it on the blackboard. Writes in chalk how
much a studio apartment will cost them. They laugh.
You know that? They laugh. She wants to make
a difference. Val, can I call you Val? It's serious
enough. Serious enough they don't think I'm crazy.
Behind us a line has formed. It loops the concourse, back
through the double glass doors which open, close, open.
I am vaguely aware of my body hunched over the counter,
the veil of airport heat hanging over us, of the way she slides
the boarding pass and a free drink coupon to me under
the palm of her hand, like a precious gift.

Layover

Ed on a barstool in the Phoenix Airport says, am I boring you? He notices the way I watch his crooked pinkie when he raises his glass. Says, a dog bit me. So I shot it. Is that a self-help book you got there? Divorce? I'll give you all the help you need. Two years. Two years and it's over. I'm gonna retire in five. I want to sail. To be served. Says, I hate books. You spend time with them and you can't put them down. He bought 300 acres in Arizona once, sight unseen. A real estate agent drove him out to it. It took hours. There it was. A pasture like a desert plain. A rock. He sat there for six months beneath the Arizona sun. He built a 3600 square foot house then. Built the whole thing himself except he needed help, once, with the logs, trees rolled out for a roof. He says, my hair back then, it was longer than yours. One year it took me. I'd done it. I was ready to move on. I get up to go and Ed says, yeah, that bitch bit me. So I shot her.

Boarding a Flight to The Underworld
with Sisyphus

We can't get to the gate
Because someone suggests
We go to a bar. So of course we do,
Bumping against each other
Like tourists ready for a river cruise,
Rolling our baggage up and down the concourse.
There is another bar too, one with a slide.
Maybe one after that,
Our bright coins dropping across countertops,
The runway outside
Glittering with rain.
The gate agent, backlit by dazzling light
Looks like the one-eyed ticket taker
Who cheated your mother at the County Fair.
And when he tells you, finally,
You'll be seated in 2C sir,
You turn to me and say,
I forgot the passports.

Hawks Meditating at Esalen

for Diane di Prima

Two red-tailed hawks circle the blue plane
of water beneath my window.
They have come from the green
shadow inside the canyon
for no apparent reason.
They are not fishers
by nature and, so,
do not dive or even
descend, just this
ballet of the circle they draw
over and over. Now
there are four,
the four corners
of a parallelogram,
fluid shape and line
a continuum turning,
unturning,
holding the space.

Whale Watching at Esalen

Somewhere in late April
a grey whale and her calf
are leaving the birthing pools
of Baja, making their way
north, past Esalen.

All day I watch the hump-backed rocks
in the sea, waiting for her.
At night in my bunk I think of the way
she hugs the shoulder of the coast with that calf
gulping dark mouthfuls of silt and sea light,

breaching the black surface,
wet stars rolling off her back, how
she is compelled along five thousand miles
of Pacific floor

by this wordless thing the calf
has awakened inside her.

I've Been Wanting to Tell You

Last night you were standing in the field
by the house. I forgot to ask
what you were doing there, in the uncut hay.
It doesn't matter. I've grown used to
finding you like this, beside the barn
or next to the pump house,
arms at your sides, looking at me
as though from a Victorian photograph,
your stillness always something less
than death. Last night the moon
made your skin the color of cooled milk.
Or marble. I think it must take a lot of love
to become flesh again. I've been wanting to tell you,
I have a son now.

Like the Sleep of Dresses
on Warm Bodies of Women

from a line by Mark Strand

Like the sleep of dresses on warm bodies of women
your room quietly folds around your absence
awaiting your return. The bat, scarred glove,
board game pieces toppled to the floor,
a book tucked inside the bunk bed's ribs
and flashlight hidden beneath a pillow
that still holds the shape of your crown.
Your dog curled into himself—head to tail
like a rich red fur collar—
keeps watch over this small country.

Like the sleep of dresses on the warm bodies of women: excerpted from *The Sleep*,
collected in *Reasons for Moving Darker*, (Knopf, 2000), by Mark Strand

The Trial of Stones

My son drops three wet stones into my pocket.
They are small songs falling against me, black
stories waiting
to be told.

Today   the City   gleams.

In the light of rain something affirmative has occurred
between us.
I watch him with the red dog, knee-deep in turning surf
Does water **affect** *stones?*
stay   here   safe

The address we have is not the one you would have chosen
        I know
it rains too much but the rooms are full
of light
for writing.   Coverage and abundance.
Throughout the streets the sodden shapes of broken men
sleep in door wells just like ours
everyday.

Stretched out in the bath
my child has grown.
Placing each black stone into the warm water with new respect
Will you write it, how they have no souls?
and begins to tell
the other story, the one from the galaxy unseen.

On the windowsill tonight stones dry
give us each their old silence,
still
we take them out of the storm waters of the Pacific,
ask them to speak.

Scripps Pier, 1965

(*Fiat Lux*, Ansel Adams)

for Kent

The day the girl next door got married,
after the fancy reception where
you drank your first G&T
and watched your parents slow dance,
your best friend is waiting back
at the house in his Woody.
You take the 5 straight to the beach
and surf until the last piece of sun is gone,
watching it roll back over the horizon
like a lazy eye. The pilings of the old pier
are lined up like wooden soldiers,
their shadows tall and thin
across the waves, one after the next.
It makes you cry now
remembering the color of the water,
how it poured over you like gold,
the way your skin cooled in the night air
like being reborn each time
you emerged.
You know the draft is coming.
But the boys who won't return,
they're still here.

Finding Proust
at the Homecoming Dance

for MBH

It wasn't the sweet crumb of the Madeleine dipped in tea.
For this girl it was Youth Dew perfume from Woodward &
Lothrop out of an hourglass bottle with a tiny gold bow cinched
at the waist. A black cocktail of scent which, when poured out,
brought on a heaven so heavy with longing I imagined no boy
was immune. Dabbed at the wrists, spritzed liberally behind
kneecaps and onto the small bulge of the pubic bone, just
as *Glamour Magazine* had instructed, it preceded me all night,
parting the crowd at the punch bowl, hanging voluptuously over
my head, sinking deep into the amygdala. The lavender gown
with the spaghetti straps. Shoes died to match. Like the deliciously
firm seashell shape of a cake. It was my body in that dress
standing under the disco bulbs for the first time with Donna
Summer telling us it was already the *Last Dance* and a boy
hanging off my shoulders like dead weight in a pale blue
leisure suit. I remember, exactly, as though floating above
the cafeteria, over the homecoming court sprayed with glitter,
the hot little Christmas lights, the first time I saw each
of the days lined up ahead. Watching them spool out as far
as I could see. This night. Then the next. All of the empty
white calendar squares chalked out, waiting their turn to become
the past. The night with its own perfumes yet to be discerned,
turning out, revealing itself, already gone.

Theatorium, Mount Carmel, PA

The photographer is a ghost now
hanging from a point high above the screen

from where he took the picture in 1920,
so that it's as if we're falling

into a submerged ship when we come
upon it for the first time, canyon-deep,

a room whose marbled walls draw
us down through grainy light,

into the empty seats below
gleaming /glossy, sunk

into their rows of six,
the show yet to begin,

my grandmother's young body
a ghost now too,

her long fingers playing
for Valentino, for Louise Brooks

in the velveted dark
while the empty mine shafts sleep

outside these walls,
waiting for the music of factories

to play again,
turning out

cigars/stockings, knitting
time with silk,

miners' hats, shirt sleeves and collars—
all of them plowed under

and sleeping too
beneath asphalt laid

for a drive-thru bank no one
uses anymore—

fists full of anthracite shiny
as black stars stuffed

inside their darkened pockets,
the Susquehanna flying south

beneath the Allegheny while
the world spins.

Nectarines

Creeping along these desert floors
my shadow is thin as a moth's wing.
I seek out courage from memory and want
to be sliced open
like the nectarines we sucked
along the county road,
our flair of burnt dust
trailing hot behind us,
the blood red flesh torn
from the pitted center,
overripe and fragrant,
vulnerable
in the open car.

Salamanca

It happens when you least expect it.
A boy is making your sandwich
somewhere in a small and dingy
take-out. You are tired. Very tired.
You point out the ham you want,
the cheese, and through the thick
refrigerated glass you see him for
the first time. A boy with large
olive eyes. The boy from the train.
In all these years he hasn't aged.
Not a day. His skin is still 20.
You never learn this boy's name
or even what language he speaks.
You board the *Rapido* in Andorra
and he is already there across from
you on the worn leather seats. You
stare back and forth. Say nothing.
For 12 hours it is Spanish dust and
moon-scraped plains while the heavy
August sun swings low and steady
and hot on the brown horizon, all
the way to Salamanca. The train
stops often. Families get on. Get off.
A mother spreads a dirty cloth
on the floor. Her children look at you
and the boy. Their faces are small
and brown and open. You share
your sandwich with him. Mountains
stooped at the edge of sky begin
to cast long lavender shadows
across the rivers. Soon it will be night.
Soon the train will stop in a pasture
thick with night sound and the scent
of alfalfa. The engineer will leave
half the train there in that field
to sleep among the cows, while
the other half continues south.
By some miracle you awaken
and understand this. You wake
the boy then, your hand cool on
his shoulder. It is the first time
you touch him. You step down
into the loam, the broken wheels
of your heavy college suitcase
groaning on the tracks alongside
you. He is still there in the morning

when you arrive in Salamanca.
The boy behind the counter hands
you the sandwich. Back at your
office you unwrap the layers of paper
from the stale slices of bread,
grow older as you eat.

Strategies for Getting the Message Across

First he threw away her books.
Every one.
Then he threw away her great aunt's rocker.
(He had never liked that she was Polish.)
Finally, he took the pictures from her growing up,
the albums her mother had sent out to make her whole.
He threw these away too,
but not before cutting each
with a pair of shears she'd bought at Bed Bath
& Beyond. After ripping out the carpet
he left three things for her to find:
a pair of silk wedding slippers, slightly scuffed &
a single baby shoe, brown suede.
She knew what he meant when she found them.

The Prince of Webster Street

You walk through the bright rooms repeating,
your luscious melon breasts
because the words feel marvelous in your mouth.
Blackberry-muskmelon-mellifluous-salamander-fox-fire.
Words are pearls you trade for chocolate. I do not
send you to your room.

You ask if the devil is real, your face wet with rain.
Saturday the windows steam with your breath.
Clouds are light dodgers over slick streets,
winter a new continent in your hands.

If you have another baby mama I will climb the highest building
                                        in New York and jump.
Would I be dead if I did that?   I scrub a pot in the sink. The house sighs.
I want to see the ball drop in Times Square
Take me mama and never leave me   never
leave me for another.

A man crouched inside a door-well on Buchanan
calls out to you, "Beautiful. Beautiful." A man smelling of sweat
and garlic presses his fat belly into you on a bus,
whispers to your yellow hair, "Boy, you are beautiful."
You smile, politely, tell me later, you cannot *see* beautiful.

In the doctor's waiting room we are paging through an eternity
of *National Geographic*
when an Inca prince jumps out at you from the dead.
In a schoolyard in Ecuador you push away the gravediggers,
the archeologists
and dip chewed fingertips into the hollows of his eyes,
                                        the cavity of his nose tracing
the paper-thin, fire-blue feathers still pasted to his skull.
You ask, how did the baby whose bones are curled up beside him die?
A living child's football rolls into the open grave.

At night you dream the shark dream again,
the water so black and deep it scares you more
than the moonlit cloak on his back,
teeth gleaming like knives. I am there this time, you say,
only not as your mother. Someone else. Yes. I say.
Hush, hush, we are almost there, Jonathan
we are almost there.

Outside on a Tuesday in November
a lunar eclipse is dressing and undressing the moon's face
in silver-red and flaming pink fires, a thousand sunsets simultaneously
falling across the Earth
All for you
All for you

A Kind of Joy, a Kind of Singing

It's hard not to feel
A kind of joy riding the cable
Car up California Street on
A summer evening,

Work falling away,
The little louvered widows
Opened to the August sky,
The clatter of metal and wood

A kind of singing inside
The street canyons, the tourist
Families turned out, happy as if
On a theme ride rolling 9 ½ miles

An hour under squares of bay
Light, the sadness of fog
Having lifted,
Another kind of joy.

And the Grip
Pulling the six strands of steel
And nineteen wires of rope
Up from the street,

The great cables humming
In their trenches,
Home calling from over the hill,
Another kind of singing.

California Tanka

i.

In our room today,
June light enters hard & fast,
French doors open like arms.
We lay in bed head to toe
Like shoes in a box, slick with heat.

ii.

Last night you came
In the form of a red dog,
Beloved red dog,
Eyes brimming black as pearls.
I hold you inside now like a secret.

iii.

Ash falls over streets
Like white petals dropped from trees
In last summer's storm.
Now winter comes on like summer's fire.
Will it ever rain again?

iv.

I am the river
Who longs for the moon in your kitchen
The bowl of your voice
Cupped inside my hungry mouth.
Set me a place and feed me, darling.

v.

Alight on my Rothko print
A black & yellow mud dauber
Inspects the blue & red plane
With the care of a new lover.
What secrets do we share here?

When We Were 15

Your mother is young
on a red kitchen stool.
She tells us
her flesh rots at night.
I have never heard
of such a thing.
You already have your period
show me how
to use a tampon
pluck my eyebrows
sew a straight seam
inhale
without coughing.
You are born
into
the kind of body
men want
to ravage.

On an early September
morning
at 4
we slip out
your bedroom
window, walk
barefoot on wet
sidewalks
and come to Backlick Road
where we
sit down on
the double yellow
lines and play
cards.
Just one hand
because we can.
Not a car in sight.
Two hours later
a thousand sets
of tires will roll over this place
launching
the suburban day
like clockwork.

Your father will
drive me home
in the phone company
truck, will pop
a warm beer,
in silence.

In 2 years
8 boys will crowd
around a bed where
you lie
stretched out
and lovely
fighting
for their turn
to rape you.
You will separate
your thoughts
make grocery lists
hear voices
from the ceiling
calling to you
in foreign tongues.
You will refuse
to see me
stop speaking
altogether
will move into
a foster home
where a son who
moonlights as a plumber
will take you to bed
and marry you.
All before we graduate.
At your wedding
I will stand in a small chapel
among strangers.
A single bridesmaid
will float past
chewing
gum.

continued

Lola, I come back
to this year over
and again. The
trees that night
uttering their last
summer sighs.
Street lamps
are pools of light,
the bubble of
our world
darkened and emptied
of everyone but
you and me
the sound of cards
shuffling
and unshuffling.
The next 30 years
are there in our hands.
Never closer.

The Corpse Speaks

They are getting ready to take me
out the back when someone yells,
the front door! The Irish way! A hand
smooths the bed. The dog runs off
with a slipper. My arms open as they lift
me, stiffen like wings. I will not
fit the door. And so it comes to be that I leave
this place as I came into it, feet first and turned.
There, I see you lingering on the porch
as they carry me out, the weight of your son
in your arms an anchor. I told you once
I was born on a night just like this one, torn
from a cowl, its gossamer netting translucent
as spider silk. See here, two men in black satin
coats zip the vinyl bag and carry me to the dark
hearse, its engine a beating thing puffing plumes
of exhaust across the yard like breath. You
are wailing like a child in a great white desert,
snow swirling around your skirts. But I hear
nothing now, only the hole of your mouth.
The chestnut trees above you clawing the frozen
sky seem to say, this has all been done before.

The Things That Are Left

Sonoma, 2018

for Bob Puccini (1947-2018)

Six months after the fire
The hills are no longer black.
They have been working hard all spring

Pushing out the new growth
In increments so small and mighty
You'd think they were burn patients

Learning to walk again.
Even the angle of light
Crossing their stubbled faces

Is raw. The hull of a melted car still
Smells like escape. The brick
Chimney standing in a field

Of weeds is writing a song
About irony. They talk about the
Rain as though it will wash

The charred pine green again.
The timothy grass finds this amusing,
Its laughter

A golden switch in the brittle
Wind. They watch us
Breathe in the perfect molecules

Of the dead. Like this glass,
Tipping it forward, drinking in
The color of autumn light.

Excerpt from a Brief History of Fire

We could end up dead today Billy told herself as she strapped the baby in.
A power line had arced over the City behind them, sending a bolt

of blessed mother blue into the sky and a shower of light onto the dry
land. The Eucalyptus stood and shivered brilliantly for a split second, then

combusted. She thought, It is the first time a landscape has betrayed me.
The flame in the village below pulsed like red lava and she'd already been

down on her knees twice to pray. Next door the neighbor was watering
his roof with a limp hose. Smoke had not yet sucked itself up the canyon

chimney in front of their house but they'd been warned when it did it
would be too late to run. The highway was etched below them, carved

between the sea and cliffs. It glittered with headlights in the fog of fire,
and the wind roared in her head. Billy thought, my child's mouth will fill

with dust and will empty of language. But Don was still stuffing
her car with shit. Clothing she hadn't known they had. Beach towels.

Dishes from their wedding. His fraternity paddle. And he said, or she had
understood without him saying, The baby rides with me. Billy had thought

she could live with this in time. She'd never had a baby before. The way
Don would put the car seat up front so he could touch their boy like a

rabbit's foot. How could she explain it? She had thought she could adjust
when he said, "You can have the next one." She knew he'd been kidding,

the way she knew it when he told her he'd shoot her between the eyes
if he ever caught her with another man. Billy was not thinking of bullets

that day. She saw the way the Eucalyptus danced in the wind in their
yard, *like witches hair,* she whispered to her baby as she breathed him in.

Don told her the plan. He would follow with the boy, they'd meet
at the bottom, and Billy thought, We don't have time to unpack this.

Or maybe she thought, He's the father of my child. I trust him, still.
Either way she pulled the car out of the drive and joined the caravan

of evacuees making their descent to the sea and as she drove
she thought of the miracle of rain when they first moved here,

how it had come up over the canyon like a wall of water,
awakening a thousand sleeping frogs from the dust who then kept

her awake for weeks with their repetitive song. A rainbow had emerged
tentatively out over the ocean one afternoon, arcing clean over

the canyon, terminating impossibly on a patch of grass at the end
of their street. She had run back to the house to get the baby then

and had placed their hands inside the colored vapors of its tail.
Had she imagined her entire life up till now?

The great machinery of putting out wildfires rolled up the road
beside her and she saw that the faces inside were battle weary

and soot-smeared. She would read about the fireman who would die
two roads over but she could not say if she'd seen his face that day.

What she'd tell you she remembered was looking for Don's car in the rearview mirror over and over again, of getting out of her own car and standing

on the metal-hot roof, of seeing the world back-lit by fire and filled
with people who were not her boy, of coming home two days later

with both of them and finding the house intact as though nothing
had changed.

Welcome To Algiers, Ma Chérie

(1984)

after Elizabeth Bishop

Here we are. "*La Maison Blanche.*" It looks nothing
Like a white house. It's a ruined little airport by the sea. Backdropped by

Scruffy hills. Stained marble floors inside and a kiosk announcing
Direct flights to Moscow and Minsk. I had not expected Russians.

Here come the Saidi cousins! Two carsful of them marching toward us,
All speaking at once. They are embracing my companion Salim.

Vigorously as though he has returned from war and not just his waiter job
In France. I hear his voice falling in among theirs, his boyhood tongue,

The deep dive into the throat song of Berber and Arabic mixed
With French as the colored bags go round the carousel,

The French words, pedestrian to me in another place, bubble up here like
Bursts of light—*Diner.* Ah such a comforting word after a day of travel.

Where will we be dining? *Les Etats Unis.* Oh, that's me! They're talking
About me now. The girl from *Les Etats Unis.* A spatter

Of incomprehensible words, then, without warning, *Poisson*! Yes. I know
That word too. How marvelous it is to hear it! But wait.

Do I look like a fish standing here gasping for water?
Is that what they are saying?

The girl cousins are saying goodbye, are air kissing each other and I find
Myself in the car with Salim and cousin Amar. I sit alone in back,

Like a visiting queen. We are speeding, the two Saidi men and me,
Across macadam toward the Casbah. Do they pave these roads?

Look up, girl. There are red flags, green flags waving
Joyously. And the sea.

I've never seen anything so deep and blue in my life. I sling
My arm out the car window to feel the air on my skin. I'm in Africa!

The men in front turn to look at me and I roll it up.
We are pulling up now to a hotel – "*Le Havre Alger*"

Wedged like a hardened French pastry between
Crumbling cakes that used to be villas. These are all a blotchy pink,

Overcrowded with voices and bodyless laundry hanging in the late
Afternoon sun. We are riding up the hotel's spiny lift now.

Salim has begun to rub his thumb over my hand, speaking rapidly
To Amar. The little key in the lock clicks, the door swings open and here —

We have the room.
Ah, the room is rather grim.

Electric fan. Sullen teapot on a table.
The window does look over some buildings and over them a lozenge

Of sea. They are speaking to each other again, sentences that twist
And labor over the bed.

They are being careful. With their words. I see.
We cannot stay here. In this room. Together. Because

We are not married.
It appears Salim has miscalculated our lodgings.

Right. They are looking at me and speaking again to each other.
Oh, daughter of adventure, is this to be your lot, to be discussed by men

Like a beautiful problem?
Sit down on this corner of the bed. It's firm. Breathe.

Okay. We're driving again in the car, me in the back again. A decision
Appears to have been made.

I can taste the salt in the air now. The windows up front
Have been rolled down for my benefit. The red and green flags are drawn

High over the *Boulevard de la République*. A lighthouse blooms
In the distance, and here we are,

Salim's house on the edge of the sea.
A white façade and a small dog in chains.

A fresh cousin has arrived to give me
Something.

The family has gathered. There are many of them.
They are smiling.

Cousin whose name I have lost track of is reaching out with
A gift. Ah, lovely. It is a package of toilet paper. Pepto pink in little

continued

Perforated squares, for me. Can this day get any better?
Of course it can. A lesson next on how to flush the toilet

With a bucket of sea water. Someone (a cousin?) is handing me a *Tisane*
Now in a cup with a saucer. The tea is the color of pale mint

And its steam fills my head. It is perhaps
The most beautiful cup of tea I've ever seen.

Who among you thought of the toilet paper?
I want to say, thank you very much, *Merci. Merci beaucoups.*

Surname

Paris, 1985

What do you know about blue zones in the afternoon? It is spring two weeks after your twenty-second birthday and you are in love with a man who owns a fine restaurant and, as it happens, a big car. You intend, mean to be just a moment, a pause, a dash out of that car, into that restaurant with its starched white linens on tables, the scent of lemon and saffron like a microclimate in your head, some small errand to complete. You are a caricature of a girl in love in Paris in a light blue frock who has colored her hair. And you have parked the car. What do you know of blue zones and uniforms?

•

They arrive, as they often do, in a car, this one compact, dark and hard as a bug, the kind of car you'd imagine in a movie with subtitles and a high-speed chase through the 6th or 7th in hot pursuit of a jewel thief or drug dealer, the *pin-pon pin-pon* of a foreign siren ringing out. Except there is no need for sirens here. No chase. Simply a parked car in the blue zone at three o'clock. That is all. They arrive dressed in shiny-brimmed képas and boots, of course, high polished with laces, their small steno pads and Bic pens drawn from their pressed breast pockets. You run out of the restaurant, bright key in hand, the way you'd seen your mother do back home once when they tried to tow her Buick. You approach these two in their starched pants and shirts fearless in your textbook French: Good day. Please may I move the car? Have you tried the food here in this fine restaurant? The bouillabaisse is quite good. Your smile is large. Here we have a beautiful blue car with white leather seats and seven speeds parked in the blue zone at 3 o'clock. Here we have a girl in a pale blue dress with a smile. These uniforms are very polite. They smile back. Do you tell them, girl, it is his restaurant, too? Do you say his name then, feel it turning inside the red flannel of your mouth like something suddenly foreign?

•

What could possibly be wrong? You hand them, these two *flics*, the registration from the glove box because they ask you for it. Though even you find this odd for a parking citation, they seem harmless enough beside the large car puzzling over the document like a small piece of evidence. It is spring and you would like to stay on the dappled sidewalk in the warmth of this day, to take in the plane trees again along the Boulevard Montparnasse, their pale green branches so in love with the sun. You would like the story to turn here, to go back inside, to sit awhile with your lover at his table over tea and profiteroles scented with orange, his specialty. But you are driving now down the wide boulevard in the shade of those trees and your lover who has worked his way up to this city from the deserts of Algeria is sitting in the back seat of his own beautiful car wringing his hands while you, a girl in a blue dress and colored hair drive with a uniform in a cap in the seat beside you and another behind you in a black car has turned the flasher on and its lights are cutting ribbons of red and blue and white into the afternoon.

83

Colorful Architecture

Paul Klee, 1917

They say every moment he could get
during the first war
he devoted to his work.
At thirty-eight,
his friends newly dead,
the Army handed him a brush, an apron, a scaffold
and told him to paint camouflage on planes,
beautiful German machines they built to roll over
words like Arras, Cambrai, Ypres.

One eye sees, the other feels.

Every   moment   he could get

Opened in the still July air at lunch
a box of watercolors
slings the moon green across paper,
a moon shrouded in half-penumbra
like a mauve-colored echo
of itself—
eye within eye,
a deconstruction of pain,
the blocks of Tunisian light from the year he spent there,

napping in the afternoons on a linen sheeted bed
the scent of curry, coriander hanging
ripe as sex,
the dog rustling its chains below the shutters.
I remember what it was like
to be loved there on a hill,
the hill like a fragrant afterthought in the blue eye of the Med
the lungs full of light swallowed after a three-day dust storm
left me housebound
with no one who spoke English.

Was it this way for him?
The weight of life's architecture needing to be recalibrated

laid bare and clean on a plane,
days when it's just too difficult
to focus,
when you find your keys
in the fridge
behind a bowl of forgotten noodles and a box of cheese,

that instead of juice you've packed
a beer in your blue-eyed boy's lunch box
which he opens in the *plein air* of the schoolyard
and that is why the phone is ringing now,
why the keys are cold,

the massive beauty of this world shredding
light into windows
rolling it up into sleeves of blue and russet
faceting away the black
and triangulating the gold,
the little houses capped like birthday hats
on a late summer day,
the drawing no longer a drawing,
something else.

Modi

(Fr., Maudir, v., to be accursed)

Anna Akhmatova
pencil on paper: Paris, 1911

— AMADEO MODIGLIANI

And I will turn to marble also.

— ANNA AKHMATOVA
In Tsarskoe Selo, from *Evening* (Kneller, Boston: 2013)

I

Birthday Letter to My Son

Eugenie Garson Modigliani
Livorno, 12 July 1906

My beloved vagabond. You flew out of me
on a midsummer's night like this one, twenty-two
years ago, hands full of stars you'd carried
with you, eyes popping open for the first time
to the curve and arabesque of my body, a map
to be savored and recalled.

You have long known the story
of your birth, the creditors' fists at the door that night.
They could not touch a woman in the passion
of her labor,
so your father piled
all that we owned
onto the bed with me, and as I cried out your name
you entered this world between chair legs
fur capes, silver
pitchers,
and gold coins, like a tiny king,
our fortune saved.

My darling son, I pine for you in Paris.
Do you think of me? Our trip to Amalfi?
You painted the sea the color of my own eyes
and laid down the terracotta and dove gray
of Italy like a seductive paste. I hear
you sketch women now in the cafés of Montparnasse
for money. I pray
you are keeping
well. I enclose
a small draft
which should
defray
the cost
of paint.

Your loving mother,

II.

Postcard from Tsarskoe Selo,
February 1911

And what was god-like in Amadeo only sparkled through a layer of darkness." [1]

— *Anna Akhmatova*

Brother, lover, friend:

Verlaine taught us there is beauty
in what decays.

I think this must be true
even in love.

People will ask one day what happened.

I will tell them this: I was 20 and it was summer.
A bouquet of roses tossed (thrust?) into your open window from the
street below. The Impasse Folguière. You found them
upon your return that evening, arranged so exquisitely across the floor.
How had I done it? This act of magic without a key? You always asked.
Afternoons beneath the sweet darkness
of your ancient umbrella in the park. Reciting each of the verses
we so loved while the chestnut trees absorbed the Paris rain intently.
They were listening to the beauty
that grew into us, so inseparable were we
the gardens seemed brighter for it.
I have hung the sixteen portraits of my body you gave me
upon the walls of my room. Today I live
like a widow, fields beyond these windows blue
in Russian moonlight, deep with snow. You said to me:
On communique – Il n'y que vous pour réaliser cela.
We understand one another. There is no one
                              but you that makes this happen.

Brother, lover, friend: Does it matter who you have been to me?
In January I was still yours.

---

[1] This quote and the story of the roses Akhmatova tossed into Modigliani's studio in the Impasse Folguière, are from *Memories of Modigliani by Anna Akhmatova*, first published in August 1964, *London Magazine*, Vol.4, No.5 (*translated from the Italian by Bernard Wax*). The reference, in French, to *On communique – Il n'y que vous pour réaliser cela—* is also from this interview. The line "In January I was still yours" and "widow" in "Postcard from Tsarskoe Selo" are references to untitled poems in Akhmatova's collection, *Evening* (Kneller:Boston: 2013), dated Spring 1911 and February 10, 1911, respectively, written in the months after she left Paris and returned to Russia.

III.

Ghost of the Sleeping Nude

Nu couché (sur le coté gauche), 1917

$157 Million for a Modigliani Raises Hardly Any Eyebrows

— *NYT, May 14, 2018*

Perhaps he will be the most famous artist of them all. [2]

— *Anna Akhmatova*

Look at me! How I fill the canvas with my flesh.
How I dominate the space we made together,
his brush to my feet, my very own arms and calves,
the curve of that glorious ass! He did me
justice.
O, how I loved that body.
Think about it.
A louche like him, paid 15 francs a day by some rich guy to paint me
in the nude.
And a hundred years later there I am, being auctioned off
for $157 million bucks.
Can you believe it? I mean, what would that buy him or me in 1917?
For 5 francs a day
I did that painter's bidding on a sofa, table
floor, anywhere he'd tell me to cross
or spread my thighs. And I did it without fear.
You can see it in the way I look out from this picture
my hair cropped (I cut it off on a dare, left it behind on a train), my head
twisted over my right shoulder.
Confident, you know, in a fuck you sort of way. It was transactional
our time together. As plain as geometry the painter and me.
I'd heard about him on the street,
how he called himself "modi"—as though he were some accursed
character from a poem.
He liked to take off his clothes at dinner parties for effect,
and pull women by the hair, he liked long hair, liked to bang
their heads into the iron gates of the Luxembourg Garden late at night.
Not my kind of date but they say he had a certain
charm and I think I know what they meant,
the way whiskey opened a hole in him that let in
the light.
I wish I could tell my mother.
A fucking private collector, can you believe it?
Look at me, hanging over some Chinese billionaire's bed, watching
over him
doing whatever rich guys do
beneath a gorgeous nude.

---

[2] From *Anna Akhmatova and Her Circle*, Compilation and Notes by Konstantin Polivanov, translated from the Russian by Patricia Beriozkina, The University of Arkansas Press (1994), "Emma Gershtein and Nina Olshevskaya-Ardova, Conversations," p. 152.

IV.

Portrait of Jeanne, 1919

Look at me, Modi. Do you see me?
I am wearing the white blouse my mother gave me,
My belly swollen with our child.
You are dying as you paint me.
I am dying too.
Do you see me?

The painting is officially titled, *Portrait of Jeanne Hébuterne (1898-1920).*

This Is a Picture of Alexander The Great Feeding Some Birds

from a fourth-grade history report

The illustration reveals our subject in a private moment.
Dressed in purple-crayon shorts and matching beret
he's got bright yellow balls for shoes
and a mouth like a tight red line drawn south. He looks
worried.

His arms are outstretched in a cross, dropping
what could be stars through stick fingers.
The birds have yet to arrive,
the diamond shaped pellets continuing to drop onto the page.

Across the top in teacher perfect cursive: This has nothing to do with
Alexander the Great.

I want to ask, really? Did you see Thebes burn? The ash of the citadel
blown across the Aegean like brain fog. And behind you
the 17 cities you've named for yourself, falling
like sons you'll never kiss. Who doesn't want
to feed something?

It's no cake walk to the end of the world and the Great Outer Sea.
Your parents, they want to kill each other, and this is all there is—
a flimsy purple raiment between you and the world,
a few breadcrumbs in your pocket,

and nowhere to retreat, your face stamped
onto every coin and cornerstone of the empire.

Even the feet in this picture already
so weary of life's campaign they're reduced to yellow orbs
we might rub like ancient lamps.

Few have known
he played the lyre as a boy,
carried a book of poems into battle.
That he loved his mother.

Can we not believe even the Great
can be undone
by a stroke of beauty?

Grant Avenue

Walking home tonight from work, as I've started to do now that the days are longer, I realize I take the same route every time. Up the heavy hill of Sacramento, across Battery, Sansome, Montgomery, Kearny. The rush of traffic on my right, past Henry's Hunan, shuttered now after the lunch crush. And always left onto Grant with its vaguely familiar odor of incense and grease, as though I am trailing something I cannot quite see or articulate, the snap of paper red lanterns strung across the street bouncing on their invisible threads and currents of air. Since I've been doing these walks I can't recall a night where I haven't come down this street. My mom brought me here when I was 16. It was the first vacation we ever took together, the first we could afford. She was younger then than I am now. I wonder if I am half-searching for a store where she bought me a jade ring. The stone in that ring was pale green and oval, flecked with something dark like truth. I wore it on my right hand through two more years of high school, an abortion and senior prom before the stone fell out one afternoon and I happened to notice the ring, still there on my hand, like an empty claw. Instead of telling her I had lost it, I threw the gold setting away. What compels us to keep such things? Tonight the sudden flash of a blue and white vase in a window feels like summer. A leather faced man is playing a two-string fiddle on the corner of Grant and California as I push through the tourists. I wonder if they know he is really only playing B-I-N-G-O or if it matters that the Chinese slippers piled in the doorways to the shops are polyester now, not silk or even handmade anymore, because the sound of his strings on the old wood is so forlorn we can pretend we really are in China or that this place exists as something more than it is. The brick and mortar shadow of Old Saint Mary's spills over the sidewalk like a ghost, and his fiddle case as I walk by is split open, to a gash of red velvet strewn with coins and dollar bills. Still on Grant, I cross California, down the hill, the store windows filled with jade carvings and gold, sunglasses and plastic suitcases. I pass through the concrete dragon gate where two strangers in long dresses are trying to hand out copies of the *Watchtower*. I turn off Grant then, onto Bush Street and the City where I live now feels suddenly cool, fog emulsifying the Bay light. I notice the way the trees along the street seem to light up my path home, the way their veined leafy linings from underneath as I walk seem afire in green with flecks of gold.

The Man Who Forgot His Baby Daughter

comes home at night and heats a can of soup
over a small blue flame. He sits alone in the dusk
of the rented flat, breaking saltines one by one
into the indifferent broth. Wife gone. Car
repossessed. All that's left is a name. He stares
at his hands. Smooth white hands that have never
dug ditches. Hands that played music once,
built things from nothing. He did not mean it
this terrible thing he cannot undo. Her face floats
in the crowd on a random street corner. She is grown
she is half grown. She is small, so small she fits
inside his hands. At night when the moon
crusts the window he stares at the white of the ceiling
and asks nothing. The voice that calls to him
on nights like these tells him, again, she's not here
so insistent he must look again in the back seat
where she's been all along, all day while he worked,
just sleeping, her eyes closed, the faintest trace
of spittle on her still-damp chin, strapped in
as he'd always done to keep her safe.
How does such a thing happen that a man
wakes up a man and goes to bed a broken
thing? He thinks to himself, tomorrow he'll sweep
the floor, open the blinds. That maybe it's not too late
for fresh-cut flowers on the table, to swim naked
in a cool river, to open his hands and ask.

The Evaluation

They arrive for coffee and pastries
promptly at 10, the tall, tennis-
tanned sentinels of the country
club. You really want this, you tell me.
I've baked, vacuumed, squeezed
post-partum hips into acceptable
slacks for you, successfully completed
the wine and cheese episode, followed
by the dreary cake and tea thing
in Brentwood.

As you go on about your shiny new
baby, pointing out the newly purchased
ocean view, I sit in your dead father's
tattered chair, transfixed by the sudden
hole in the dish cupboard window.
The menorah, Seder plate and dreidel
I gave you, gone. Their familiar shapes
stenciled out on the undusted shelf.

Across the startled space
your eyes are simon-pure.
They say, we can pull this off,
can't we?

First Death

Skipper died today.
Your father found him first,
one fish-eye fixed downward
toward your sunken pirate ship,
the other cast out
through the pattern
of fingertips and nose prints
into the sea green depths
of your room.

We circled the bowl, speechless
in the face
of a small bloated body,
lustrous red
in the morning light,
dorsal still undulating
voluptuously
on unseen current.

Your first impulse,
to reach inside and touch
the open gills.
Your next,
to squeeze shut
your eyes, reopen
and look again
at each of us--
the bowl,
the room,
your own small hands,
as though, like me,
assessing
the new
world.

Maryland Crabs

Two dozen hard shells arrive today
cold and dead. You fly them in from Hagerstown,
our summer celebration. Twenty-four red backs
line the kitchen counter. Giant porcelain spiders
on my pink Mexican tile. Forty-eight hard black
eyes steamed eternally open. They stare at the ball game,
my Limoges in the cupboard. Enough for us both,
you say.

You sit alone with your mallet, your bottle of beer,
shuck them one by one. A slight sucking sound
of vacuum sealing. A certain Chesapeake smell released
and I remember the flesh was sweet. How Old Bay
would seep and burn and season its way into spiny
finger-tip wounds. The tincture pink stain
on my palms. When I could sit back and say
I was full. Satisfied.

Sucked out and hollow. How these sharp
little legs and claws scratch beneath the skin
and snag the heart like memory. Red hot July
days with your daddy on the screen porch. Orioles
on the radio. The hum of locusts moving thick
through humid Eastern air, that slow and steady
engine in the back of your head. Days before
you even knew my name, when we were nothing
more than a bright red promise.

Fable

The possum fell into the black abyss
of the trash can last night. Tipping
a conical nose in for a look from the edge
of the neighbor's wall, her claws
slipping right over the plastic lip.
She didn't know it was empty.
I listened for hours, to her
scratching to get out, clawing up the sides
of the can, a low growl just under the wind
until 6 when my husband, the brave one,
who takes the spiders out of the tub
in the mornings, my son nodding his jelly-
stained cheeks, *It's hard for mommy*,
takes the old broom from the house
and knocks the can to its side.
Then, waiting a respectful second
for the exit, half expecting a nod of thanks,
peers into the gloom of the can and is
taken aback, insulted even, by the flash
of sharp little teeth, the small black
lips curled back hissing and that guttural
sound. *I can't believe it's growling at me*,
to no one in particular. Then, in sudden
appreciation of the peril in which he has
surely placed himself, jumps onto the hood
of the old white car and straight on up
to the roof, all six feet four inches of himself,
a safe enough distance from a possum I guess,
unless they jump. You never know. Then,
brandishing his broom in a great arc-like
gesture, in his ridiculous terry cloth robe
with one arm half missing and his long toes
hanging over the top of the windshield
says, with all the authority of a large
woman perched on a very small chair,
Shoo. Shoo. This must have done it
because the possum walked right out
of the can at that very moment,
dragging her prehensile tail behind
her and sauntered back into the wet
underbrush, making apologies
to no one.

Moon Diver

The fire alarm goes off along with the power
the night your stepdad is away. Sleep-heavy,
you follow me down into the lobby depths
of our new home where we stand in pulsing red
light, me in his oversized rocket-ship pajamas,
you in Sponge Bob and disarm the thing together.
Beyond the front door cars submerged in the City's
great night river move past in dream-slowness,
lapping their lights against the tempered glass.
Your small dry hands fall limp at your hips
and I half-carry you upstairs where the boys
in 2-B are drinking gin fizzes and playing scrabble
by candlelight, their door open wide. A face
humming Cole Porter floats up from the hallway,
places a small diver's lamp around your head,
"for the journey home." Back in the big bedroom
where the wolf moon splits its blue web against
our window, you are gone to me completely,
the silver bubble of sleep between your lips
rising, falling, your eyes dancing beneath
their perfect lids, your lamp a small bright orb
to carry us both home.

Now We Are Six and a Half

Your humor is getting to me. The way you pop
out from behind walls, doorways, appearing
suddenly from underneath beds like a blonde
jack-in-the-box. Little pixie boy. *Ha! Boo!*
Did I scare you? Nothing is sacred at six
and a half. I'm pulling up my pants, just off
the toilet, when you burst in with an *I gotcha.*
Or an ice cube down the back of the poor
man who wanted to take me to dinner.
The now famous phone cord pull incident
when I was on the call with the client
from London who doesn't like children
and should never have them. And the long
beautiful elocution with the plumber who finds
your "guy" in the trap as I hold my breath
and listen from the hall. The morning you go
out with the dog and don't come back I wait
a beat before I am yelling your name to the morning
papers on their doorsteps, the slick backs of cars
on the empty street. The gut-sinking empty street.
I will beat down doors for you. You know this,
your name bellowed through open suburban
windows, zinging past cereal bowls and jelly toast
on sunlit breakfast tables. And then I hear it,
the tiniest, faintest, *what?* from behind a tall
blue recycle can. You and the dog emerge,
a team, bravado falling away in the presence
of my half-dressed body, one panty hose leg
on, the other dragging impotently behind,
a lump of mascara smeared on my left
eyelid. You take me in with those enormous
blue things my father gave us both, that give
us both away. Back in the kitchen you are
the one yelling, *Mamamama lemme go*
I can't breathe and, Boy, I won't give you up.

Food & Wine Rant

Bay Area Food & Wine, April 14, 2019

1066 A.D.

This Michelin-starred go-to spot in the FiDi offers genre defying concepts. Hand-crafted martinis with locally sourced cocktail onions brined in paprika from the Guadalentin Valley in Southeastern Spain (in a nod to his English roots the chef grows these white pearl beauties out of his own garden), artful flatbreads slathered in chicken skin butter with renderings steeped in squid ink, and organic kale sliders (gluten free optional). The space here is captivatingly mid-century, the service sardonic. Modern edges and sharp angles abound. The 15-course tasting menu ($345) certainly delivers when paired with a couple pours of the 1850 D'Oliveira Verdehlo ($260/glass). Go native--try the spicy head cheese and duck offal confit. The cauliflower and hen of the wood mushroom entree lacks culinary luster but hey, it's vegetarian. What do you expect? Do you want to walk away from a meal wondering about the nature of food, the universe? Life itself? Don't be so god damned precious. Who can afford this shit? For those of you who keep tabs on these sorts of intrigues I did not get the restaurant critic promotion. I toast my new boss, 30 years my junior!

Bay Area Food & Wine, May 5, 2019

Last Man Standing Brasserie

The dining zeitgeist that won't go away! This place totally shatters expectations. It's genre defying. The scooter-toting child boss is going to eat this stuff up. It's got a certain molecular magic. I keep asking myself, is it delicious enough? The Bees Wax Scented ice cream parfait is to die for! Bees wax? Are you kidding me?

Bay Area Food & Wine, June 2, 2019

Tiger Tail Pizzeria

Turns out she did not like my last review. Said it sounded like Last White Male Standoff. So here we are today at this new rising star of the Mission. And the real star of this story is the Pinsa Montesacre with organic black kale, Calabrian chilies and garum. Whatever that is. Consider it a deconstructed torte. Paired with a curated selection of ales with a 40 or higher IBU on the International Bitterness Units Scale. Fuck. It's a $38 dollar pizza. Can't we just get a god damned slice of pie and a normal beer? I would like to convey my sincere appreciation for your continued support of these reviews. I am currently undergoing a change of circumstance and am in discussions with a news distributor in the Western Pennsylvania area. Stay tuned, Foodies! Catch me soon *@food&winerant*

The Lycoming Valley Mall Shopper, September 15, 2019

Derrick's, State Highway 54

Greetings foodies! I've moved in with my elderly mother in Central Pennsylvania! We are going to get to know the food scene here and you're gonna love it. Let's start with this little gem right off State Highway 54. Video and vittles. Who doesn't love that? Ask yourself, did this menu surprise me? Specializing in Indian, Chinese and Amish food. Specializing! A nice biriyani with a dollop of chicken fried white rice and a bottomless glass of Dr. Pepper. Man oh man I should've made the move back home years ago! Catch me next week on *Food & Wine Rant*-- Time to rethink Cracker Barrel? And how do you like it best? The top shoo-fly pie spots— wet or dry? *@food&winerant*

The Lycoming Valley Mall Shopper, November 10, 2019

The Sticky Elbow

Foodies! I am now writing to you from inside a Starbucks inside a Walmart because my mother's cat peed on the internet cable and shorted out the house. Truly. This dump smells like vomit and Clorox and three kids are simultaneously screaming for lattes. So let's talk about the Sticky Elbow today. No spiritual vibes of the tasting format here folks. And the tableside spectacle? Kids! In highchairs. Boosters. And they throw food too. My recommendation? Just order the goddamn pizza. With some little nitrite flavored pepperonis for the kiddos. Next week a double delight! Locally sourcing your scrapple and how to get shot out of the bird before the Big Day! *@food&winerant*

The Lycoming Valley Mall Shopper, December 31, 2019

Chez Maman

Foodies: Sending you love and nostalgia as we ring in the new year this evening from my mother's 1950s kitchen. Do you remember those avocado green blenders you gave your moms in 1968? Time to pull those classic babies out of their obscurity in the back cupboard. I am living proof they can turn out a mean smoothie: 1 part ice to 3 parts vodka. Enjoy! And here's to a brand new year. Bring it on 2020! *@food& winerant*

Pheasant Season

The girl watches her grandmother from the cellar steps, watches how she plucks the quills like daggers of feathered silk, from a still-warm body. Upstairs the men pull off their boots, pour out their mugs of whiskey and warm their red hands by the stove. The girl knows nothing of what came before except her mother's leaving and her father's absence, sharp as a point. The old woman chops the head off and pulls the blade clean through without a sound. The same tight silence she gave the night a hunter shot her brother through the heart. The woman thinks about the color of the bird in the moment before it fell in the field, of how much light a girl carries in her eyes, what she will make her husband and this girl with what she holds between her hands now. Her shoulders soften, shaking slightly beneath the bare bulb as she raises her hands over the soft, pimply flesh—here is the seed in the gullet, the single undigested blade of grass, the velvet wound, the startled blood spilt across the white sink top. As if to say, this, my child, is all I have to offer.

Northumberland County Crossing

A train runs over me
still, in this lost place where dual rails shine
like currents of summer light across Old State Road, nothing more
than a dust line dream now, drawn East
through cornfields that form the thinnest point

of all beginnings and ends
of me. Once a day a somnolent turning of steel
rim on iron comes on sleep heavy
from the South, no longer stops here or even slows
but recalls

a reason. Like the wheel that paddled
millstream through air and light, still
as a clock face no longer keeping time,
or the mill itself
emerging from sedge,

hollowed as an old man and shuddering slightly
through broken window eyes
in the wake of the old engine's
northbound passage.

The Boy Who Was Hunt

for W.H. Hastings, once known as Arthur Leigh Hunt

How can I create for you this world I share with the dead?
Can we start here, in the room I share with the living? Blue all around
like the sea in summer, white shades lifted to allow
moonlight in,

a small red dog asleep (reluctantly), my lover and I spooned
into restless pandemic dream. Imagine next the curved corner between
bed and window, pressed weightless as shadow against the wall:
our guest, my guest really,

not so much uninvited as unexpected, garbed as he is
in the woolen uniform of another time, dough-boy hat in hand.
He comes here as his once 17-year old self, scrawny, bespectacled.
I think the dog sees him too,

this boy who was Hunt, a runaway so without
all his boy-life he wore his mama's shoes to school. And when he
recovered
from the virus that terrible year,
still bleeding from eyes and ears, the without
became so much more,

and no money for college. He is a boy who knows his mother
will not let him go,
a 17-year-old who has a plan: with a hasty flourish of ink he mints
a new identity,
invents, then forges

a new name, moves back
his birthday one year to the day,
to join a war over by the time he enlists. I want to ask him,
Do you know how this single lie will open

the door to the rest of your life, close
all of the ones behind you, forever?
He touches his new name beneath his buttoned coat
                                        as though he hears me—
the letters etched onto a pair of silver dog tags, stamped

like a mnemonic device around his neck.
                        It is a name he has lifted like a stroke
of brilliance from the blue seaside village of his father's birth, a name
with its hiss of s's, and sting of sound,
the name of a famous battle, my father's name, my own. A name

that will ensure no one
will find him, until I do.

Since March he has arrived each night in the hour of blue dusk, each
night like the first: a repetition, a narrative he has invented in which I am

complicit. You might well ask, why does he come, now?
Let us follow him as he leaves the house on 21st Street in Oakland
for the last time on a June morning in 1919, his mother upstairs asleep,
the boy not thinking at all about how often she will call out

his name in all the days and years after, not thinking
of the brother, who will search his whole life to find him, but
never succeed. Does the boy soldier in my room know
                                                these are things I know?
The boy who was Hunt, who is becoming my grandfather, boxes up

all memory of these people, takes
the shaded side of that familiar street as though already hiding something,
his head bent
downward as he walks away
as though memorizing the placement

of each pebble, each
blade of grass, its perfect color that morning --
or is he merely repeating his new name, shaking off the weight
of mother love in those first steps? In five years time

this boy will have seen battle like his new name,
will be offered the privilege of four years at West Point, will
graduate into that long blue
line, First. And even years later,

when he becomes an officer in the United States Army
                                                he will make certain
the photograph is
of his profile, never his face.

Does the boy come here each night because I know his secret?
Perhaps it is the constant chant in my head which goes on at all hours
now but especially at night, *please
protect my mother save my father my son my husband my grandchild
                                                my sister my brother, please*
that has drawn him out, brought him here like particles of dust

continued

carried from the past, re-formed in this blue space
that is my living, into the shape of my dead.
What then does he think of this small ménage? Our raucous
fighting and love making, our daily living   our fear
of dying?

Let us follow him again as he travels
from the bedroom to the kitchen. Does he marvel at the Viking
stove with its six burners, the healthy

hum of the fridge as he examines the plentitude of food
in the freezer? Does he pull open
the silverware drawer,
consider the knives and forks and spoons in their formations?

Does he really leave behind
no print, no trace, except
the protestation of the dog each night on her bed, fur on end, tail
between the legs, low growl in the throat? As he ambles

through the house does he wish to remove
his costume, lay ghost naked in the deep
pile of carpet and become
his boy self again?

Or to touch the surfaces of photos of his own sons on my desk?
You may well ask how I know he's with me. I have no choice
but to appeal again to your imagination.
Last night he whispered, I am sure I heard it,

I'm sorry I frightened your dog.

Camp 5b, Niigata

for John F. Breslin, M.D. (1908-2003)

You come to this place locked inside the cargo hold of an unmarked
POW ship the Allies strafe with bullets. On the open sea
                              you cut out a man's

appendix with a bowie knife, a finger of gin, the guards hunkered down
with a single oil lamp to see the American doctor work. This is who

you are. The man you've always been. In Niigata the snow is three feet
deep and there are no shoes. No medicine. No heat. You work with bare

hands, a few bottles of quinine, quietly rotating the ones closest to death
off work detail in the mines, the foundry, carrying them in your arms,

laying them down like the children you've left behind, on mats of straw
and paper. You drink weed soup, eat wild garlic where you can find it,

and worms. I study your face in the only photograph you bring home.
Rows of men in black and white lined up against the odds of unheated

barracks in the Northern Nippon winter, their bellies swollen round,
shadow of bone beneath skin. You stand out even here in a tattered coat

a preacher named Perry O. Warren traded you, the initials "POW"
stenciled on the collar, your jaw clenched, 85 pounds thin, eyes

darkened deep inside their sockets, Errol Flynn mustache intact. I'd know
you anywhere. You are the same man who will walk me to the school bus

stop in the Pennsylvania rain after my parents' divorce, singing *Buffalo girl,
won't you come out tonight, come out tonight,* the one who will smash

my record of *Auntie Mame* against the Hi Fi in a rage and hide in the cellar
sobbing at the sound of thunder. The same man who will walk me down

the long aisle of my first marriage and drink away the dark of a thousand
nights. You, who risk everything one winter night beneath the camp

flagpole, the dead light, taking the coronet the Red Cross sends, bringing
it to the lips that would kiss and bandage my roller-skated knees to play

Good Night Sweetheart, the notes dropping over the white emptiness
of the camp, the men and the guards, all of them, falling silent together,

as though hearing music for the first time.

The Five-Year Old
& The Ghost of The Holy Spirit

It is always November that year in Pennsylvania, my feet still numb
in their faux-fur boots, my father at war & the absence of my mother
constant as a phantom limb.
Sunday we'd ride from the Church of the Resurrection
like the four horsemen of the apocalypse—
me, my grandparents & the ghost of the holy spirit—
the homily, to which my grandmother would listen (her fist
curled against her breast), hanging over us in the car home
like all the months of winter weighted in a single day.
A doctor who survived three years of a Japanese POW camp,
my grandfather believed in God, the perfectibility of trees
& Manhattans before dinner.
In his absence
my grandmother raised three daughters alone in the town next door, got
her girls to church
in a red wagon once a week, cleaned, plaited, ironed and fasted.
Neither of them knew
I drank holy water in my bed at night.
If they'd have asked me then I'd have said I didn't know why.
I knew
my grandfather hid in the basement when the storms came up over
the Allegheny that year, they slept in separate bedrooms,
that on Sunday we gave thanks
for the fact my grandmother cooked just one meal.
It was a meal of love & obligation certain
to contain eggs & scrapple in gray shapes on the plate, slabs
of bread & reminders of starving children in darker places
than here, reminders she would not cook again that day.
And because of this fact it was also the day of the week
I did not have to sit alone at the dinner table
after the light had gone out over the trees in the yard,
to finish every bite, the day neither of them drank.
Shattered plates danced back into their cupboards and talk
turned to more polite conversation
about eggs & pork & bread, how Father Weichert managed
a good joke over coffee in the church basement that morning.
It was, also, always the day
we hiked to the deepest & darkest place
on their farm, a hardwood forest that had grown up
in the time of a revolutionary war, a place
where the trees leaned up high against the gun metal sky
and our feet sank into layers of leafy mulch. Where animals
left silent footprints iced over like small cataracts in frozen mud & snow.

My grandmother carried cherry cough drops
& Parliaments in the pockets
of her suede coat, my grandfather
his toothy red hand saw,
which he wielded calm as a surgeon among the elm,
seeking out the saplings, carving off their lowest limbs, & perfecting them,
in his mind seeing them grow straighter & stronger, the fallen limbs
of boys still fresh
in his mind.
I already knew
there is not much constant in this life,
but there was this.
The sting of November on my face.
My toes numb in my boots.
And something like the holy ghost walking
                      with me in the November light.

With Best Wishes for Our Happiness, March 22, 1932

after Peter Handke

I open the book, *Plays – Ibsen*, and find my grandfather's inscription to her: Like a ticket stub stamped in time: The beginning of a story; A play: My own: My first death, my second mother, my third eye, with eyes in the back of her head till the end, the woman who fed, dressed, walked me to school each day drilling times-tables into my seven-year-old brain, gave me God every night and each morning,

on my knees, who swore me to NEVER MARRY AN IRISHMAN: All those long nights around the kitchen table in the rural wasteland where he'd bought a farm after the war, forks scraping the blue and white china in the half-lit silence, the certain silent shape of her back over the stove cooking in the heat and in the cold months; the old room worn out from years of such silences: Did I ever see her — *happy?*

My grandmother: dead now 35 years. Like an investigator opening the yellowed pages of an unsolved mystery, a crime that may have OCCURRED, as opposed to one HAVING BEEN COMMITTED, one that OCCURRED in the past, in the PASSIVE; like an outside investigator, in my own way, I would like to represent this one life, as exemplary, a series of choices available to women of a certain time, indeed,

a *richness* of choice resulting in a REDUCTION OF HAPPINESS, a kind of BEAUTY BY FORCE. She played piano in all the big houses as a teen — Victoria, State Theater, Theatorium in the little coal town of Mount Carmel, certain to leave open her leather boots, their buckles FLAPPING madly as she worked the pedals, laying down cover for Chaplin in *Gold Rush* and Garbo in *Flesh and the Devil*; she told me, once

They called us flappers. How she loved it, that act of defiance in the shadow of the theater, a kind of FIRST HAPPINESS made to be coaxed, fanned along like a small fire, the flammable images on the screen lit up, bright with the kind of life certain TO HAPPEN TO her, and wasn't the music she was making with her hands and the soles of her very own feet its own kind of happiness, even as she buried her mother

at 16 — a mother given over to her own surfeit of choices, suffering a stroke in one of those same theaters on a Friday evening at 50, the Phantom in *Phantom of the Opera* too horrible to bear after bearing a dozen children, brains of the family meat company, quick with numbers and pregnant her whole life — her father a dutiful husband already grooming the housekeeper to be the next bearer of his seed (a girl our subject would never acknowledge as her sister). In 1931, she moved to Washington to BECOME twenty in those last heady days of prohibition, learned to dance in basement bars in the District, some with music she dreamed of playing one day on her own piano, started nursing school but fell forward into her destiny instead, the burst of fire in her body, all of it happening so

quickly, marrying into an Irish clan, his family never forgiving the beauty that had seduced their favorite son, never forgiving her for GETTING HERSELF PREGNANT – 35 years later she would tell her first daughter, on the occasion of her husband's promotion, just before the big toast, CONGRATULATIONS! that she had tried to abort her with a coat hanger — a second girl came one year later: In the throes of labor she named her

Ann, before falling into that deep medicated sleep they gave women of a certain time, and upon awakening was handed the child her husband had named Mary, the name already typed out on the birth certificate, a done deal as they used to say. A third girl came next, followed by a fourth after the war; and even after all four daughters had finally moved out, one of them dropped

off her own girl, age seven, a cruel stork trick, to raise up *for a year or so;* and so it came to be that first summer when the cat showed up after a week in the fields to have her kittens, my grandmother drowned them each in a tub in the basement, all but one, the most beautiful of six, which she gave me as a gift, never saying where the others had gone, so that later, much later, when I was TRYING TO BECOME

pregnant, I dreamt of the sound of cats scratching at the cellar door, trying to get free, of babies drowning in the bath upstairs in that old house. My grandmother taught me to play *Heart and Soul* on the piano, placed pieces of anthracite in my pockets which I held on to like black magic, like precious crusts of stars fallen from heaven, drove God deep into my lungs, helped me pen letters

to my father in Viet Nam even though she didn't speak to him, taught me math each night at the table before the evening meal, and told me, more than once, *I hope to live to see* THE MAN YOU MARRY: Which never happened, except IN MY DREAMS. In time her piano stopped playing music except for the banging of random notes by her many grandchildren who sometimes came to visit.

Orpheus Spinning

What would I tell her now?
That I've learned how to balance
between two worlds, one light the other dark?
To look forward and back
as though through a mirror?
In the weeks after it happened
I must have swallowed a dozen pills
watching the reflection of myself
doing it over and over again in the mirror
as though trying to see my body
beyond itself, sleeping,
only to awaken
with the same absence
like a hand slipping
back into shadow.

•

Darling E,
I've started spinning at the Y with Sisyphus. You should see
us, our chiseled bodies perched on flywheels
that go nowhere,
calves
hardening like blocks of marble & music
so loud I think it's a drug meant to stop the singing
in my head. Sis cranks the tension all the way up all the time
so that he can barely move the pedals, both of us becoming
more like ourselves every day.

Do you remember that last night
in the west field? How the acacias laid down their bright arms
to my song, the stones lifting from the warm earth to dance?
Sometimes I think bad things happen because we're meant
to be someone else's destiny. You
are the memory that pushes
through calf & bone & muscle.
The first time I thought I saw you
here, through the sweat-fogged mirror, was like a bolt
of light in my chest.
We keep doing the same things over again.
I miss you.
O.

•

She rose up like heat from
the stony field, her cherry-dark hair
more dazzling than light off
the mirror of the sea.

•

I don't recall the specifics of that night.

You know, Plato always said it was a set up.

That girl.

ruined.

my reputation.

Are you going to take advantage of my story too?
(Interview with *Vanity Fair*)

•

She submerged into the five rivers of darkness,
the way fog emulsifies air,
an apparition.

It was a set up.

•

The last thing I remember?
Her face, of course.
I sang her out of hell.
Who wouldn't have looked back?

There Were No Witnesses

This may come as a surprise but "down here" the internet is on fire
& every search of "Eurydice" comes up "Orpheus."
"She stepped on a snake." "He looked back." "Their myths cannot exist
without each other." Bull shit.
Which was precisely
what you were best at.

He was a victim of her beauty

In those early days of grief you really worked this story, O,
belting it out in dim concert halls, mesmerizing the crowds of wolves
alongside the wild deer
& gulls. I could half-believe it myself. Except
I was with you before all that, inside
those years spooling out ahead of us.

How many nights did I lay awake counting the electric tick
of the beside clock, widowed by your midnight gigs,
creeping back to me at 4 or 5, reeking of other women's charms,
cigarettes & sour sweat, your voice hoarse from all that singing?

In the bathroom Sundays doubled over
your spiral notebook & the toilet, writing the lines of your next sure hit,
not emerging again till sunrise, dinner spoilt.

Don't even get me started on your mother.
Those high-minded poetry readings in her living room where no one
could sit on the furniture, tossing back alliteration & consonance
like so many dry martinis. No woman good enough
for her golden boy, son of a muse. We hadn't even finished unwrapping
the wedding china when she started in,

Coming round in her tin-baked crown whispering
about my past, playing you
with her magpie tricks,
slutty dryads insinuated into our story like the bad
sequel to a bad Plath poem.

After that you saw suiters everywhere.
In trees. Bushes. The produce aisle at Safeway
for gods' sake. You began locking me in the house, the bathroom,
the closet. Tossed out my favorite flowered gowns. Put a tambourine
in my hand, told me
to play *pretty*
in the background.

What did all of it get you in the end
but a   good   dead   girl   story?

That night in the field I saw what you did, Orpheus,
the way the stones came to life from the black earth, the trees
swooning to your voice beneath the moon's white eye—

Did you really think you could blow
in my ear and I'd follow you anywhere?

Did you know

My mothers were many
in a glade of oaks that sprang up green
& brilliant in the wilderness,

That I learned how to wear darkness & savor the music of the dead
because I had to?

Look ahead now my darling, & beware.
My bones are scattered in a field &
angry beauties with voices of their own are coming.
They are rewriting the myth even as I
dissolve
like dream
behind you.

To the Stranger
Who Sexually Assaulted Me

Let us start again, slowly this time.

First, recall the night:
>>>dark/early autumn/rain-slicked streets
>>>a small unlit park at the intersection of 6th and Mass.
>>>a half-drunk girl in a leather jacket walking home alone.
Do you remember it now?

I remember

you wore sneakers, the sound they made on the wet pavement, the way
they slapped like something angry and pushed, a sound that came rushing
up behind me so fast I hadn't put it together with your body until our
bodies were suddenly slammed together and I began fighting for my life.

Slowly this time.

The force of your body is your only weapon. I know that now.
I can feel the muscle of your shoulders draw me down, the small pattern
of concrete on my face,
the night reduced to the bare elements of your hands,
the scent of rain, the distinct taste
of the salt on your fingers in my mouth.

Do you marvel as I have over the near perfection of our communication?
How we knew in those moments exactly
what we wanted, what the other wanted,
the only words spoken the ones you whispered in my left ear like a secret:
Don't scream.

Dare I say after all these years I know
I was your first?
It was your technique that gave you away
all impulse, unprepared
for my whole body rejection, rude elbows, fingernails, sharp little suede
pumps and, of course, the scream
you'd asked me not to make.

I see you running away from me now, that your sneakers are white,
how you stop and turn and look at me from across the street,
the curtain of rain beginning to fall between us
and I want to tell you something:

You entered me in unexpected ways.
Sometimes when the wind blows against my back it makes a sound like
feet pounding toward me and my heart jumps back inside my throat and
my head spins around to look behind to see who's there.

116

Slowly   this   time

I *see* you, for the first time—your head turning to look at me from
across the street, the way the rain falls like time between us, that the color
of your eyes is brown.

You wanted something from me once.
You see, I've come here, now
to take it back.

Seven Days at Old Saint Mary's
During a Retrofit

i.

First: behold
the air arc welder. Blue
fire & stars
falling through the open roof.

ii.

Madonna is on her side leaning deep into a pew.
Yesterday, a massive painting over
the altar. Today just another woman
trying to get it right.

iii.

An electric saw splits
cold air mixed with the weight
of incense.
I pray out loud. No one
can hear me.

iv.

A homeless man, bathing in holy water.

v.

They've moved the *Pieta* outside
to the lobby. You can glimpse her from the street now through open
doors, her bent frame
trying to cradle her dead child,
daylight pouring over marble.

vi.

Jim attends the welcome desk and tells bad
jokes. Very bad. But they're not dirty
& you miss him when he's gone,
a handwritten note propped up
in his place: *Prayer candles $2. Please
do not bathe in the holy water.*

vii.

Last: a gathering of small fires,
shy in the open space, they
are the votives
sent to join the *Pieta* in the lobby,
make a small rushing sound
as of red silk in a current
of air.

Disaster Tourism, 47 A.D.

(*Things Lost and Found at Pompeii*, Science Museum of Virginia)

Pearl earrings suspended behind glass. Pearls pulled from oysters pulled from the sea, the sea as it looked then. A surround sound reenactment of the pyroclastic surge of poison and pumice narrated by Pliny the Younger who, it turns out, spoke with a British accent. Head-phoned families, mouths agape. Villas splashed across a screen, mountain lurking behind like a villain, the inevitable darkness. A 2000-year old loaf of bread held up like a trophy on a plinth with spotlights, the crust perforated, still, into eight equal portions. A living child's nose pressed to glass. Fishhooks dangling in curated light. A golden snake bangle curled into itself holding out for the familiar bicep. The same way the earring remembers the flesh of the lobe. Drinking cups and dipping bowls made for sauces we might make at home. Sunburned shoulders pressed together at the diorama. An egg keeper like the one in your own fridge with 6 empty oval slots. A dozen amphora with swollen bellies and rounded lips dreaming of wine. A contraption for drinking wine while lying down. *I think I'd like that* someone laughs. A bronze bathtub like an open casket. Scales with carved faces of lions made to measure out food, gold, the day's joy. A bronze speculum, opened. The shouts of parents: *Oliver! Logan! Get back here. Mason. Do NOT push your brother.* A coin left behind. A guard suppressing a yawn. The screech of a stroller wheel. Perfume bottles laid out like time capsules guarding ancient molecules of scent. Teenage faces lit up by I-phone light. Red toenails poking out from summer sandals beneath the marble body of a goddess, her own white nail beds perfectly moon-shaped. Ochre. Cinnabar. Clay hewn from lava fields. Memory. Ash. Heat. Oxygen. The warmth of a boy's hand trapped inside a glass prism gifted to him by his father. Displaced sun dials. The wrist watches of their time. Chestnuts. Black walnuts. Another coin. Apples painted onto paintings of glass bowls. Mirrors that still give a semblance of truth. *Gaius was here* scratched onto a wall. A boy asking his father, *what's a speculum?* Casts of once human beings. A young man who shields his face in his arms, enslaved to the end. One pants leg is drawn up over his rounded calf. His naked ankle, the lines in the foot still indelible. Beside him the blurred shape of a woman burrowed into the ground. A pillared courtyard where time and space in an endless loop reveal a three-legged table holding the weight of a bowl of plums. Outside it's still Richmond, Virginia in 2019, and the day feels like it's encased in amber.

Like a Holy Bullet

for R.B.F., 1941-1998

Your death began its journey in September,
the month of apples and honey.
Carried on that first note
of a ram's horn,
it arrived one week later
on Yom Kippur
as I stood beneath a white tent
and struggled
with a new language I had married
to say your Kaddish.
I fasted the news,

your name,
a claw of hunger
that shot clean through the book of life.

At the Little Church of the Rock
your funeral was stadium-sized,
the young minister coaxing to convert
just one more
in your memory,
scripture in PowerPoint flashing over us on wide screens
and then a snapshot of you
in a rowboat
holding a half dozen of the biggest fish I had ever seen
in your fist, plunging them upward.

"Do you know where you'll be sixty seconds before you die?"
Your own voice, hidden wizard-like
rained down over us
as though you had pre-arranged it,
a direct satellite link.
And as we pondered this riddle
the show suffered an electric glitch
a sudden high-speed frenzy of photograph/Word/fish/Word
that flashed and bounced over the congregation, unleashing
in me
a wild urge
to laugh
or dance

except
the image of your widow alone
on stage in her trim blue suit
radiant
diminished
in the sudden void
of your departure,
stopped me
cold.

Sailing to Fallujah

(2004)

The sun this evening moves over
the Pacific, a fog bank compressing,
flattening its familiar shape into
something long, almost cornered.
As it bears its great orange weight
down upon the sea,
its colors thickening,
the bow and stern of a small ship emerge
and take its place,
a tiny, gold ship
like one of those perfect miniatures in the British Museum
housed in glass,
a miraculous artifact from Babylonia.
It is a pre-Christian
pre-memory ship
that leaves a giant V in its wake.
As it glides, sideways, over the arc of the Earth
slipping out of this day
it is rising simultaneously
in the East,
over Fallujah,
the white minarets,
over the children in their beds,
over the men and boys with guns,
and the tanks that wait, spilling
its gold into the streets.
I want to call it back then,
to fill it with mothers,
mothers who have lost
their sons
their daughters
to war
from the beginning of time—
that army
unstoppable.

What the Heart Wants

The Christmas tulips have opened
Their red cups.

Assembled in the vase, they
Announce the end of something

I seem to have missed.
My mother never came.

In the house today—
A sudden scent of wood smoke, tobacco, damp wool

So familiar
It knocked me to my knees.

Who can say they know anything
Of the life of the heart?

Except this--
It wants what it wants.

Red Pine

for Hilda Beatrice Breslin, 1910-1985

Death first came to me
at twenty-four.
It came hushed and thick
and pine-scented
along the snow routes of Europe,
whispering your name
somewhere between Stuttgart
and Kitzbuhel.

That night
all night
I stared at a picture window filled
with mountains
that led me back to Germany, Pennsylvania, Kentucky—
all the houses that wore you down
like the clothes you took to wearing
mended and re-mended.
They hung on your shrinking skin
and billowed around you
until you were nothing more
than threaded shadow inside them.

Death came to me
two days after Christmas
in a frozen month
that blocked all the roads out
and kept me from your funeral
while the scent of pine
followed and pushed
forward, insisting
its way home
then stayed on
in all of my rooms
long after you were planted in the ground.

The Morning After

The first memory is the morning after.
It's the woman with the basket on her arm,
long black coat, red scarf.
She slips along a snow path in soft grey light,
into the Austrian village where I have phoned home
to learn you are dead.
I am naked in a chair where I have not slept all night.
Before I have learned to drink this away
she disappears beneath the window
three days after Christmas,
unaware of the smallest ripple your life has left.

Dreaming to Kathmandu with My Son

We are somewhere in China. A walled city that looks down upon a river. Elaborate boats are moving below us, gorgeous in water light. Red boats outlined in real gold leaf that shimmers the current. Their shape is strong, curled up at the bow and stern in carvings I cannot make out from the river's edge. We take one of these boats. On board the river air rushes past, is cool. I am nervous about the money we have brought, about the foreign language. There is lunch to be bought, vegetarian noodle entrees and leathery chicken salads. I buy the vegetarian. We share this, my son and I, on the boat. Later, I stand alone at the mouth of the river beside my divorce lawyer. He tells me he has ordered the leathery chicken on the boat and it was awful. Just awful. There are giant department stores around us, models with silky black hair who stand in the windows. They are adorned in fabulous creations, each more sumptuous than the last. I am aware I have no money. I say to no one, I have no need for dresses. My lawyer will buy one for his wife. Then I am together again with my son where we began, at the river. We turn our backs to the water and face a white staircase that leads to Nepal. The stairs are a pure snow-glazed white. We go, hand in hand, beginning to climb the steps to the great city. We cannot see it from where we begin, but we know it is there, above us, lustrous as a dream.

Moth

Tell me, you who are born without mouths,
how do you make your music?
Is it lovemaking you have come to study before you die?
What do the iced blades of moonlight in the scrub oak teach?
And you, noble pantry moth, wings like grey ash
on my skin. Do you wish
for goodness when you lay
your small brown eggs
inside my bag of flour, your mouth O-ringed
in white dust or does duty
urge you on like a kind of bliss?
Small brown flutter in the dank closet
feasting on my blue wool dress: What do you carry
with you? Is it the same crash of stars these celestial
bodies circling my porchlight seek tonight?
Do any of you covet
your celebrity relations—
those raucous monarchs flying into extinction
in their great orange-black swarms?
Do you begin each day with a prayer to life?
O, glorious silkworms in the mulberry tree
that grew beside my window—
fruit gorged, bodies fat with green
bursting from your glistened pods,
silver-threaded wings of childhood—
the trees are dust now. Where are you, where
have you gone, today?

Anticipatory Grief

The road back is five hours of gunning past trucks on the turnpike
in a downpour and then: the roses she planted by the gate, the first

of so many to come. An early frost pulls the green off
their fragile black limbs, tears open their hearts in a red burst

you pick for her table. Later, through the open window of your once
childhood bedroom: hawk, wolf, wind call to you, again, in ancient verse

while the ghosts of all you once loved tap dance on their brittle toes
behind the closet door, suckle your breath and slake their thirst

for the living. A train's air whistle cuts clean through some dark field out
beyond the road's edge where you can almost feel the way the worst

of this will come. Down by the barn descendants of dandelion greens
you devoured so long ago have overgrown the path,
                                                        you imagine rebirthed

each rose your mother planted. Here, far from the house the wolf pup
leans into the wind and howls for love, the dark one she knew first.

128

Sunshower Over The Rappahannock at My Friend Ann's River House

A quiet so still even the mosquitoes are listening. Soft skittering
of pebbles over water.   Applause.   First in the leaves of trees.
Then clattering between the margins of riverbank.
A storm rising over my grandfather's field in late summer.
I run inside the green light of that memory
in bare feet, hair plastered to my face.

It is the same fat ball of joy between the ribs.

Even our eyelashes are glittering. Pinballs of light
striking our faces like tiny meteors. The fish
in their green kingdom below are watching our reaction.
Each drop on the emerald surface is the element
of a new periodic table being written for the first time.

As though the child I was has time travelled here, to this
circumference of light. To be astonished again. The tongue
in my mouth feeling the roof of the river's mouth
for the first time.   All that is left that is still good in me.

The simple truth of heat.

Even the dock has noticed. As we sit here cross-legged, on its bones,
rain lashed, our butt cheeks warming, the sun reaches back down
like a giant yellow hand on our shoulders. While each sphere of rain
holds its own skin, each an entire universe of water
lit from within.

Ode to the Crow

Human beings are the only ones in nature who are aware they will die.
— *Paulo Coelho de Souza*

Even the blackbird knows death
is a kind of persistence:

drop stones into
a pitcher and the water will rise.

What is worth doing is worth
doing again.

Stone by stone they gather like boisterous omens
on the roof at dusk,

the rattle and click of their subsong
is a chord of sorrow built

inside a murder of joy.
These six black dancers in a circle

of rain:
how can they not

celebrate the fire in the trees
today, the flame of sun

dying against the hill?
I've seen the beloved

when they fall.
Fête my own with a funeral

of beating wings.
Conjure their dark magic with

overfilled bins of pandemic takeout—
they are so busy

memorizing our faces, seeing
veiled spaces hidden from view.

How hard this is
to resist envy of such gloss-inked

freedom: stone by stone
they are building heaven

with coal shined nails. Even the crow
knows this much.

Canzoniere

for my mother

I think by now the river must be alone
        in her thoughts, late in the day, late summer

I imagine her as she was to us that afternoon:
        shimmering green as a liquid gem in July heat, the perfect

listener as we lunched hunkered over
        our baguettes and cheese along her banks, you *on the wagon*,

again, as we used to say, drinking
        iced water instead of wine, careful with your words,

but I can tell you now I loved the moment
        you unfastened your sandals like a girl and plunged both feet

into the emerald waters of that day, a color
        you ask me to describe for you again on the phone tonight,

we were speaking about Petrarch how
        he had come to the river to write of loss

as we trace each
        meter of memory, even the waitress later that evening

slicing us a piece of each cake
        from the *chariot de desserts* because we could not

bring ourselves to say no. I will never see you
        so young again. I think by now the river

is alone with her reflections,
        late in the day, late summer,

I imagine her
        as she was to me that afternoon.

About the Poet

VALARIE ANN HASTINGS earned the Steve Kowit Poetry Prize 2020. Her poetry has appeared in more than a dozen literary journals including, *Crab Creek Review, Literary Mama, Marin Poetry Center Anthology, MomEgg Review, Paterson Literary Review, ProseAx, SheMom, The New Guard*, and the *San Diego Poetry Annual*.

She was nominated for a Pushcart Prize in 2019 and earned finalist status for the Steve Kowit Poetry Prize (2018, 2019), the Knightville Poetry Prize (2019), the Allen Ginsberg Poetry Award (2020), and the Crab Creek Poetry Prize (2011). She lives in the Bay Area.

About the Artist

LINDA HAIM MEADOWS earned a BA from Yale and an MFA from Indiana University. Her work is part of private collections worldwide.

Acknowledgements

Some poems in this collection first appeared or will be forthcoming in the following publications:

San Diego Poetry Annual: *When Pigs Could Fly* (winner of the STEVE KOWIT POETRY PRIZE 2020)
If Joy Were a Hit and Run, Love Poem in a Pandemic, Sunshower Over the Rappahannock at My Friend Ann's River House, Scripps Pier (fiat lux, Ansel Adams) [all Finalsts: The Kowit]
Geese, 1968

The New Guard: *Searching for Dandelion Greens*
[Finalist: The Knightville Poetry Prize]

Paterson Literary Review: *The Prince of Webster Street, When We Were 15, Photograph of my Parents, 1971, "Old Eggs," State of Emergency* [Finalist: The Allen Ginsberg Poetry Prize]

Literary Mama: *Like the Sleep of Dresses on Warm Bodies of Women (after a line by Mark Strand); This Is a Picture of Alexander the Great Feeding Some Birds*

SheMom: *The Trial of Stones*

MomEgg Review: *Moon Diver*

Crab Creek Review: *I Would've Had Another Version of You, That's All.* [Finalist: Crab Creek Review Poetry Prize]

ProseAx: *Between Places*

Marin Poetry Anthology and ***Clark Street Review:*** *Photograph of My Parents, 1971*

Credits

Cover: *Dandelion Field*
acrylic on canvas —9 x 12 inches

Frontispiece and section pages: drawings

— LINDA HAIM MEADOWS
@lindahaimmeadows

King Cake Baby: page 10

Pennsylvania Train Track: page 103

— photographs by VALARIE HASTINGS

Photographs of the Poet: KENT JONAS

133

Gratitude

The writing of *Searching for Dandelion Greens* has benefited from the support and care of many readers, teachers and friends including the late Steve Kowit, Rosebud Ben-Oni, Shanna McNair and Scott Wolven at The Writers Hotel, Lisa Bellamy, Rachel Nevin and Kathie Jacobson at The Writers Studio, the late Diane DiPrima, Ann Chinnis, Dana Scott, and my editor and friend, Bill Harding. Thank you for your consistent support, encouragement, kindness and, especially, your humor.

Most of all, my love and gratitude to Kent, whose constant support and belief made this book possible.

134

Made in the USA
Columbia, SC
24 September 2022

67567363R10078